Community College *Is* College

Combining research with firsthand experience, *Community College* Is *College* demystifies—and destigmatizes—the community college sector.

This practical and accessible resource presents community colleges as an option where students who have been identified as high achieving can receive an excellent postsecondary education, often in preparation for transfer to a four-year institution or entry into a high-demand career.

Covering topics such as the mission of the community college, dual enrollment, tuition and fees, transfer, and career opportunities, this book is a must-read for high school counselors, parents, and caregivers committed to providing students with a complete understanding of the higher education options available to them.

M. Beth Borst is Founding Dean of the Ivy Tech Community College Honors College, Indiana, where she is also a professor specializing in Leadership.

Brenda Geib-Swanson is a full-time instructor in the Entrepreneurship and Innovation Department at Butler University, Indiana. She earned an EdD in Higher Education with a cognate in Community College Leadership at Ball State University.

Suahil R. Housholder is the Vice President for Finance at Anderson University, Indiana. She is pursuing an EdD in Higher Education with a cognate in Community College Leadership at Ball State University.

Amanda O. Latz is a Professor of Higher Education and Community College Leadership at Ball State University, Indiana.

Samantha Lopez is the Associate Director of Student Involvement and Leadership at Duke University, North Carolina. She is pursuing an EdD in Higher Education with a cognate in Community College Leadership at Ball State University.

Sonina Hernández Mikkelsen is a talent acquisition specialist for Disney Programs. She has a decade's worth of student affairs experience, including work as a dual enrollment advisor, pre-health academic advisor, career educator, and international recruiter with institutions such as Purdue University, Utah State University, and Lake-Sumter State College.

Community College *Is* College

Destigmatizing the Option for High Achieving Learners

M. Beth Borst, Brenda Geib-Swanson, Suahil R. Housholder, Amanda O. Latz, Samantha Lopez, and Sonina Hernández Mikkelsen

Routledge
Taylor & Francis Group

NEW YORK AND LONDON

Designed cover image: © Getty Images

First published 2025
by Routledge
605 Third Avenue, New York, NY 10158

and by Routledge
4 Park Square, Milton Park, Abingdon, Oxon, OX14 4RN

Routledge is an imprint of the Taylor & Francis Group, an informa business

© 2025 M. Beth Borst, Brenda Geib-Swanson, Suahil R. Housholder, Amanda O. Latz, Samantha Lopez, and Sonina Hernández Mikkelsen

Library of Congress Cataloging-in-Publication Data
Names: Borst, M. Beth, author.
Title: Community college is college: destigmatizing the option for high achieving learners / M. Beth Borst, Brenda Geib-Swanson, Sonina Hernández Mikkelsen, Suahil Housholder, Amanda O. Latz, and Samantha Lopez.
Description: New York, NY: Routledge, 2024. |
Includes bibliographical references. Identifiers: LCCN 2024026948 (print) | LCCN 2024026949 (ebook) | ISBN 9781032386690 (hardback) | ISBN 9781032375847 (paperback) | ISBN 9781003346210 (ebook)
Subjects: LCSH: Community colleges–United States. | Community college students–United States. | Education, Higher–Aims and objectives–United States.
Classification: LCC LB2328.15.U6 B67 2024 (print) | LCC LB2328.15.U6 (ebook) | DDC 378.1/5430973–dc23/eng/20240718
LC record available at https://lccn.loc.gov/2024026948
LC ebook record available at https://lccn.loc.gov/2024026949

ISBN: 978-1-032-38669-0 (hbk)
ISBN: 978-1-032-37584-7 (pbk)
ISBN: 978-1-003-34621-0 (ebk)

DOI: 10.4324/9781003346210

Typeset in Palatino
by Deanta Global Publishing Services, Chennai, India

Contents

About the Authors

M. Beth Borst is Founding Dean of the Ivy Tech Community College Honors College, Indiana, where she is also a professor specializing in Leadership. She has spent nearly two decades focused on helping students thrive in community college as they prepare for transfer to the baccalaureate and beyond. In addition to extensive administrative experience in academic and student affairs, Borst continues to work with students in the classroom at Ivy Tech and teaches in a part-time capacity at Ball State University, Indiana, and Indiana University Columbus. Such engagement has provided her with critical insight into the educational journeys of diverse student populations. Her passion for educational access and equity both informs and drives her work in higher education.

Brenda Geib-Swanson earned her EdD in Higher Education with a cognate in Community College Leadership in 2024 and holds an MBA with a concentration in Entrepreneurship from Ball State University, Indiana. Brenda is a full-time instructor in the Entrepreneurship and Innovation Department at Butler University, Indiana. She serves as the course champion for the first-year business course with a focus on experiential learning and the impact of entrepreneurship on marginalized communities.

Suahil R. Housholder is the Vice President for Finance at Anderson University, Indiana. She earned a bachelor's degree in Accounting and MBA from Anderson University and is a CPA in Indiana. She is currently pursuing an EdD in Higher Education at Ball State University with a cognate in community college leadership, where her research interest centers around the decline and turnaround of private institutions of higher education. Mrs. Housholder was named as one of Women We Admire's Top 50 Women Leaders in Education of 2023.

Amanda O. Latz is a Professor of Higher Education and Community College Leadership at Ball State University, Indiana. She also directs the Student Affairs Administration in Higher Education Master's program and Graduate Certificate in Community College Leadership at the university. As a doctoral student, she taught at Ivy Tech Community College as an adjunct faculty member and served as a doctoral assistant for the Center for Gifted Studies and Talent Development at Ball State University.

Samantha Lopez is the Associate Director of Student Involvement and Leadership at Duke University, North Carolina. She is pursuing an EdD in Higher Education with a cognate in Community College Leadership at Ball State University. Her research interests focus on the experiences of mothers and caregivers working in higher education while navigating the limited parental leave policies available.

Sonina Hernández Mikkelsen is a talent acquisition specialist for Disney Programs. She earned her bachelor's degree in Global Communication from Utah State University, then obtained a Master of Arts in Student Affairs Administration in Higher Education as well as working through doctoral courses and finishing a graduate certificate in Community College Leadership from Ball State University, Indiana. She has a decade's worth of student affairs experience, including work as a dual enrollment advisor, pre-health academic advisor, career educator, and international recruiter with institutions such as Purdue University, Utah State University, and Lake-Sumter State College. Her research areas focus on Latinx and first-generation students, as well as academic advising practice and impact.

1

Community Colleges

The Stigma Stops Here

Often the local community college is not the high achieving student's first choice when it comes time to apply for college. In fact, many students families, school counselors, and career and college readiness staff in high schools may believe the community college is designed to provide only last-chance options for students who otherwise would not be admitted into a four-year college or university. It may also be seen as an option only for students from low-income backgrounds. Depending on which state a student lives in, the primary mission of their local community college may not be seen as compatible with a student's goal of attending—and thriving at—a four-year college or university.

Rather than transfer pathways, many think of community colleges only as places for remediation, job readiness, and upskilling. And while many fields of study at the community college do in fact lead to certificates and applied degrees rather than transfer degrees, we aim to reinform and remind readers that failure to change our perceptions about the community college means fewer choices for all students—including high achieving students and students with big dreams and goals.

While negative stereotypes of and stigmas regarding community colleges still exist, those who are employed by, are enrolled in, and study at community colleges are challenging those stereotypes and stigmas. The #EndCCStigma social media campaign started

DOI: 10.4324/9781003346210-1

by Dr. Steve Robinson, President of Lansing Community College, is one important example of this work (Robinson, 2022). We see this book as another tool in further challenging those negative stereotypes and stigmas. Community colleges are an important part of the national education landscape. As the subtitle of this chapter suggests, let us make sure the stigma stops here. Furthermore, community colleges are post-secondary education institutions. Therefore, as our book title suggests, community college is *college*.

It is critical that high achieving students understand what their local community college can and cannot provide them. Curricular options and student experiences vary widely. Many two-year institutions in the U.S. are considered comprehensive community colleges, while others are not. Comprehensive community colleges, such as Sinclair Community College in Ohio, offer general education alongside technical programs, whereas technical colleges, such as the Tennessee Colleges of Applied Technology, focus primarily on industry training and workforce development. Later in this book, we will highlight what some of these differences can mean to high achieving students.

While the history of the community college will be discussed fully in Chapter 2, it is important to note the following here:

◆ For the purposes of this book, we define a community college as "any accredited public or nonprofit institution that awards the associates as its highest degree or that offers at least one baccalaureate program but confers more than 50% of degrees at the associate level" (Kisker et al., 2023, p. 5). Yes, some community colleges do, in fact, offer bachelor's degrees. The definition we are using here is not the only definition, however. It is important to understand your state's definition. And it is important to keep in mind that these definitions vary across the nation and world.

◆ In the U.S., community colleges, sometimes called junior colleges, technical colleges, state colleges, two-year colleges, or city colleges, are primarily public institutions providing higher education that focus on certificates, diplomas, and associate degrees. Some two-year colleges are private and for-profit, but those are not our focus in this book. As mentioned above, defining these institutions can be tricky, and it is best to understand how your state *does* community colleges because each is unique. There are community colleges in every state.

◆ According to the American Association of Community Colleges (AACC) (2023), 38% of all undergraduate students were enrolled in a public, two-year college in the fall of 2020. This is quite a significant proportion of college students.

◆ After graduating from a community college, some students transfer to four-year institutions to complete a bachelor's degree. Community colleges primarily attract and accept students from the local community and are often supported by state appropriations and local tax revenue. These institutions also usually work with local and regional businesses to ensure students are being prepared for the local workforce (D'Amico et al., 2019).

◆ Since the 1960s, open access has been at the core of the community college mission. During the 1960s and 1970s, community colleges saw a surge in enrollments, which included those without prior access to higher education such as students of color, adult students, and low-income students (Navarez & Wood, 2010).

◆ Approximately 52% of all Native American, 48% of all Hispanic, 39% of all Black, and 34% of all Asian and Pacific Islander college students study at a community college, which serves as a gateway to higher education for historically underrepresented racial-ethnic groups (AACC, 2023).

◆ The average age of the community college student is 27, while the median age is 23. Thirty percent of community college students are the first in their family to attend college, and 59% of community college students are women (AACC, 2023).

◆ Regardless of the type or name of the community college students live closest to, students who enroll will save money by paying lower tuition and living costs and set themselves up for success at the baccalaureate. The average annual tuition and fees at a public two-year institution is $3,860 versus $10,940 at a public four-year college or university (AACC, 2023). Yet, even with the financial benefits, some may worry about starting at a community college and then transferring to a new institution.

◆ Transfer shock is a phenomenon where students' Grade Point Average (GPA) declines during the first few terms at their new institution. Transfer shock is a relatively outdated concept, however, which dates to the 1960s (Hill, 1965). Aulck and West's (2017) study, for example, showed very little difference among year-one entrants, two-year transfers, and four-year transfers at a large public, state-funded university in the U.S. in terms of attrition and grades. Furthermore, they found no strong evidence of transfer shock on students' post-transfer grades. More recently, scholars have taken asset-based approaches to understanding vertical transfer students. Vertical transfer refers to when a student moves from a two-year to a four-year institution. For example, Laanan et al. (2010) put forward the concept of transfer student capital, which emphasizes the strengths and assets of transfer students. This concept includes the accumulation of knowledge, skills, and experiences helpful to the transfer process— all of which can be gained at the community college. Some examples include study and learning skills, positive perceptions of the transfer process, academic advising, and attending workshops in areas such as financial literacy and professional presence.

An incredibly diverse array of students enroll in community college classes that both challenge and prepare them for all sorts of futures, including transfer to a baccalaureate degree-granting institution, which results in significant savings for students and their families. The high cost of attending college in the U.S. is well known; however, the stop-gap solution provided by the community college is often overlooked. While the community college offers degrees and transfer pathways for academically underprepared students, such as those who did not have the privilege of experiencing a well-resourced K-12 school system, it also operates on a broad continuum where high achievers can receive an excellent two-year education, often in preparation for transfer to a four-year institution and/or entry into a high-demand career such as nursing. In Chapter 6, we provide details on the reality of paying for higher education and the financial benefits of starting at a community college. High achieving students who begin their higher educational journey at the community college can save thousands of dollars and avoid loan debt.

Often these savings, along with other community college benefits, just make sense to students and their families. Additionally, because many high achieving students do not plan to stop at a bachelor's degree, saving during the first two years of college can help offset debt at the graduate level. In some cases, students may even be able to finish a baccalaureate degree at their local community college. There are quite a few community colleges that offer a limited number of bachelor's degree programs. These programs are typically offered in high-demand areas where few other four-year degree options are available. Examples of high-demand areas include Dental Hygiene and Early Childhood Education. The community college baccalaureate is available in several states including Texas, California, Washington, Colorado, Michigan, and Florida (not an exhaustive list). The Community College Baccalaureate Association (see https://www.accbd.org/state-inventory/) provides a helpful state-by-state inventory of such programs.

High Achieving vs. High Ability vs. Gifted vs. Talented

So, what does it mean to be a *high achieving* student, and how might these students thrive at a community college? Or, perhaps the more important question is, how can the community college help high achievers reach their academic, developmental, transfer, and career goals? What we know is that no two students are alike. In fact, each high achieving student will have a unique K-12 experience, which may or may not include access to, or involvement in, gifted and talented programs or colle-giate prep opportunities such as Advance Placement, dual credit classes, International Baccalaureate, Early College programs, and so on. Regardless of the diverse secondary education trajectory, high achieving students *do well in school*, and as such, they often place high expectations on themselves in high school and col-lege. High achieving, however, is not always synonymous with giftedness—though of course it may be.

Although being *gifted* is said to be related to intellectual abil-ity, giftedness may not translate into high academic perfor-mance. Literature on gifted education is plentiful, yet definitions around *giftedness* vary widely. In fact, there is much discrepancy in the way K-12 educators determine which students are labeled as *gifted* and which classes they are placed in (Oakes & Guiton, 1995). What is considered gifted depends on the school. Although achievement and ability performance measures such as IQ tests historically have been the determining factor to identify stu-dents who qualify for gifted programs, K-12 educators have been moving toward a more holistic notion of giftedness, recognizing that abilities may develop over time and in more focused talent domains (Cross & Riedl Cross, 2017).

According to Dai and Chen (2013), there is a shift in gifted edu-cation away from "alleged general mental superiority" (p. 156) to diverse capabilities and aptitudes that may develop across time. The talent development paradigm, often used today in place of performance measures, maintains that people are talented at something and that their talent in a specific area may be seen through accomplishments (Chancey et al., 2017). The movement toward talent development occurred in the 1980s and 1990s as an alternative to the traditional, single notion of the gifted child (Robinson, 2012). This model broadened the definition of gifted-ness and included diverse manifestations of gifted behaviors and performances (Dai & Chen, 2013). The talent development paradigm assumes a broader basis of gifted and talented poten-tial (Dai & Chen, 2013). According to Renzulli (1998):

> *Talent development grows out of the belief that everyone has an important role to play in the improvement of society and that*

everyone's role can be enhanced if we provide all students with the opportunities, resources, and encouragement to develop their talents as fully as possible.

(p. 107)

Some argue that motivation, drive, and grit are at the core of achievement (Duckworth & Gross, 2014). Motivation is often credited as the driver for one's ability to capitalize on talent-development opportunities (Subotnik et al., 2011). According to Jolly (2009), more contemporary models and definitions of giftedness reflect a multidimensional approach to understanding what giftedness means in terms of intellectual, emotional, and social constructs.

Regardless of the history of gifted and talented programs, we know that Black and Hispanic and/or Latinx/a/o children are underrepresented in most gifted programs (Harradine et al., 2014; Peters & Gentry, 2012). Students of color, namely Black and Hispanic and/or Latinx/a/o students, and students from low socioeconomic backgrounds are most often underrepresented in gifted and talented programs. Gifted education typically enrolls greater percentages of higher socioeconomic status, White, and Asian students (Subotnik et al., 2011). Poverty is a primary barrier to participation in gifted education programs where students from lower socioeconomic status are either unidentified or attend schools that do not offer special programming (Jolly, 2009). It is important to consider identification procedures, systemic racism, various forms of bias, academic achievement gaps, and psychosocial factors as possible causes for the disparity (Subotnik et al., 2011).

High achievers are often motivated internally and externally, which typically translates into good grades and academic success. High achieving students, whether they attend(ed) a public or private high school, large or small, or were homeschooled, may be motivated to do their best by being recognized as *stand-out students*. Scholarships, awards, invitations to participate in an honors program, co-curricular activities such as student government and student life, and membership in academic groups such as Phi Theta Kappa Honor Society (see www.PTK.org) all help motivate and drive the academic trajectory of high achieving students. It is important to note that high achievers often strive for perfection or have perfectionist tendencies, which may stymie their overall development and success in college—especially during their early years of college. Families and students might then consider a two-year honors program or other high impact program that can provide a higher level of support than is provided by many four-year institutions during these critical years. Additional information about these and other opportunities that make a community college experience a viable option for high achieving students is discussed fully in Chapter 5.

Twice-exceptionality (2e) (Reis et al., 2014) is a phrase that denotes the dual presence of giftedness and learning disability such as dyslexia, autism spectrum disorder, or attention deficit hyperactivity disorder. These individuals may also have developmental challenges and/or mental health concerns. This 2e student population may be served well in a two-year honors program where holistic advising and smaller classes are readily available. As open-access institutions, community colleges are well equipped to help *all* students succeed and navigate college, which includes services for students with disabilities.

Homeschooled Students

In 2016, about 1.7 million students (aged 5–17) were estimated to be homeschoolers, which translates to about 3.3% of all K-12 students in the U.S. (Grady, 2017). In 2021–2022, that number increased to nearly double to 3.1 million homeschool students, or roughly 6% of all school-aged children in the U.S. (Ray, 2023). The impact of the COVID-19 pandemic led to an increase in families homeschooling their children. While studies are still emerging on the pandemic's impact on K-12 education, what we do know about this population is that both students and their caregivers/parents were challenged with anxiety and other mental health concerns during the pandemic (Makridis et al., 2022). More information about homeschooling can be found at the National Home Education Research Institute (see www.nheri.org).

Homeschooled students can and do go to college, and most empirical studies show homeschooling has greater positive impacts on academic achievement as compared to students in conventional schools (Ray, 2017). Community colleges are taking note of this, and some have specific information for home-schooled students on their institutional websites. Online classes and other community college programs may interest home-schoolers who also wish to get a start on college while still in high school. Again, this is a great option for saving money and getting acclimated to higher education in a small and supportive community college environment.

Standardized Tests

While the COVID-19 pandemic prompted many colleges and universities to shift to a *test optional* approach to admissions— a trend that started prior to but was accelerated by the pandemic—others continue requiring standardized tests, including institutions such as MIT, Georgetown, University of Florida, University of Georgia, Fisk University, and others (Wood, 2023). Community colleges may require a placement exam, but they do not typically require high stakes standardized tests, which can be helpful to many students, including high achieving students who may be poor test takers and for those who simply do not have the resources to pay for the exams. Starting costs to sit for a college entrance exam such as the ACT and SAT start at around $60, and additional fees may apply. While some students may be eligible for a fee waiver, these tests as well as the preparation most students seek, really add up. In fact, Selingo (2020) reported that millions of pre-college students take some type of test-prep, which may include private tutors and cost well over $1,000 (p. 63).

For high achieving students who are not strong test takers, and/or who do not have the financial ability to pay for the high-stake tests such as Advanced Placement (AP), ACT, SAT, or College Level Examination Program (CLEP) exams, this can pose yet another barrier to admission to many four-year colleges and universities. In addition, test anxiety is more than nervousness before a test and can happen to any student, including a high achiever who may set unrealistically high expectations that add to their anxiety. Through a study examining math anxiety among high and lowachieving students, Roos et al. (2015) found that high achievers experienced more anxiety than low achievers in relation to math performance. Furthermore, many students who are neurodivergent or have learning disabilities have concerns over the College Board's move to all digital tests and the challenges students with disabilities face getting the test-taking supports they are entitled to under the Americans with Disabilities Act. According to Attorney Marci Lerner Miller, who has argued several high-profile cases pertaining to standardized testing and students with disabilities, the process needs to change to better serve students with disabilities (Gardenswartz, 2022).

Because community colleges either waive placement exams altogether based on high-school GPA or other indicators of college-readiness, or they administer placement exams such as Compass, Accuplacer, or Knowledge Assessment, test anxiety may be minimized through the community college pathway. Additionally, placement exams are offered at no cost at most two-year institutions, and exam accommodations are offered through the offices of disability services when requested. This can serve many students well, including 2e students.

Purpose and Organization of This Book

We wrote this book with the purpose of framing the community college as a viable option for high achieving students. All prospective college students should be afforded access to information about *all* their post-secondary education options. Community colleges are not often seen as acceptable destinations for high achieving students, and as such, that option may be rarely presented, let alone considered. Through this book, we argue this needs to change. We hope the information provided will be insightful and helpful to high school counselors, among others, including key information about this sector of higher education—the community college.

This book is organized into nine chapters. In Chapter 2, we describe the history, mission, and context of the community college. This is an important place to start because community colleges, like any institution, are a result of their history. In addition, community colleges differ from four-year institutions in significant ways. Understanding these differences can help prospective students make informed decisions about their postsecondary educational paths. Chapter 3 is focused on college in high school—including dual enrollment, dual enrollment, and concurrent enrollment—all terms that signify a student is pursuing college prior to completing high school. This opportunity blends secondary and postsecondary education and has bloomed in recent years. The community college is a major player in this space. There are certainly pros and cons to the pursuit of college during secondary school—all of which should be considered by students and their families.

Chapter 4 highlights the workforce education and development arm of the community college sector, with an emphasis on sub-associate credentials. This option can lead to a plethora of employment opportunities and continuous growth and development within those careers. In Chapter 5, we focus on the transfer mission of the community college and outline what the academic experience might look like for prospective students. For high achieving students who aspire to a four-year degree, starting at a community college may be a good option for a variety of reasons, such as benefitting from cost savings as detailed in Chapter 6, staying near home, and/or enjoying a smaller classroom environment.

In Chapter 7, we discuss community college student life and all the affordances of attending a community college that are not necessarily directly tied to academics yet are critical to a college experience. We discuss a variety of campus resources such as career education, basic needs support, academic advising, tutoring, and disability services. Chapter 8 includes an overview of technology within the community college environment, with a specific focus on how the pandemic has accelerated the pace of change in this area. Campus technologies are constantly evolving and having a grasp on the basics is important. Finally, we conclude the book with Chapter 9, discussing the community college return on investment and helping prospective students consider life post-community college. In this chapter we again work specifically toward our goal of framing the community college as a viable option for high achieving students.

Our book is unique. We are not aware of any other text that is primarily focused on high achieving students and the community college. We have included some additional elements that we hope are useful to readers. The book contains URLs throughout, so additional information, beyond what we can reasonably share in this book can be pursued. Also, some chapters include testimonials—stories from individuals who have experience with the community college. There is no shortage of community college success stories, and we aim to showcase some of those in this text. Finally, we end each chapter with a set of discussion and reflection prompts. We provide reflective prompts for high school counselors, college and career readiness professionals, teachers, and prospective students' families as well as questions useful to prospective students. We call the former support questions and the latter student questions. The questions for prospective students can be used in counseling and/or advising sessions or simply provided to students for their consideration.

Discussion and Reflection Prompts

Support Prompts
- ◆ Think about what you know about community colleges. Where did this knowledge come from?
- ◆ What, if anything, in this first chapter surprised you? Why, or why not?
- ◆ Reflect on your interactions with prospective college students. What messages have you sent about different types of institutions?

Student Prompts
- ◆ Have you ever considered attending a community college? Why, or why not?
- ◆ Reflect on your answer to the why, or why not question above. Are those answers based on research and accurate information?

◆ What do you know about your local community college? Where did that knowledge come from? How might you go about locating *accurate* and *relevant* information about your local community college?

References

AACC (American Association of Community Colleges). (2023). *Fast facts*. American Association of Community Colleges. Available at : https://www.aacc.nche.edu/research-trends/fast-facts/

Aulck, L., & West, J. D. (2017). Attrition and performance of community college transfers. *PLoS ONE, 12*(4), e0174683. https://doi.org/10.1371/journal.pone.0174683

Chancey, J. M., Butts, J. L., & Mercier, D. (2017). Creating tomorrow's honors education. In R. W. Glover & K. M. O'Flaherty (Eds.), *Structural challenges and the future of honors education (Honors education in transition, 3)* (pp. 13–35). Rowman & Littlefield.

Cross, T. L., & Riedl Cross, J. (2017). Social and emotional development of gifted students: Introducing the school-based psychosocial curriculum model. *Gifted Child Today, 40*(3), 178–182. https://doi.org/10.1177/1076217517713784

Dai, Y. D., & Chen, F. (2013). Three paradigms of gifted education: In search of conceptual clarity in research and practice. *Gifted Child Quarterly, 57*(3), 151–168. https://doi.org/10.1177/0016986213490020

D'Amico, M., Sublett, C. M., & Bartlett, J. E. (2019). *Preparing the workforce in today's community colleges: Issues and implications for higher education leaders*. American Council on Education. https://www.acenet.edu/Documents/Preparing-the-Workforce-in-Todays-Comty-Colleges.pdf

Duckworth, A., & Gross, J. J. (2014). Self-control and grit: Related but separable determinants of success. *Current Directions in Psychological Science, 23*(5), 319–325. https://www.doi.org/10.1177/0963721414541462

Gardenswartz, J. (2022, October 31). New online-only SAT puts students with disabilities at new disadvantage, advocates say. *Youth Today.* https://youthtoday.org/2022/07/new-online-only-sat-puts-students-with-disabilities-at-new-disadvantage-advocates-say/

Grady, S. (2017, September 26). A fresh look at homeschooling in the U.S. Blog. National Center for Educational Statistics. https://nces.ed.gov/blogs/nces/post/a-fresh-look-at-homeschooling-in-the-u-s

Harradine, C. C., Coleman, M. R. B., & Winn, D. C. (2014). Recognizing academic potential in students of color: Findings of U-STARS~PLUS. *Gifted Child Quarterly, 58*(1), 24–34. https://www.doi.org/10.1177/0016986213506040

Hill, J. (1965). Transfer shock: The academic performance of the junior college transfer. *Journal of Experimental Education, 33*, 201–216.

Jolly, J. L. (2009). A resuscitation of gifted education. *American Educational History Journal, 36*(1–2), 37–52.

Kisker, C. B., Cohen, A. M., & Brawer, F. B. (2023). *The American community college* (7th ed.). Wiley.

Laanan, F. S., Starobin, S. S., & Eggleston, L. E. (2010). Adjustment of community college students at a four-year university: Role and relevance of transfer student capital for student retention. *Journal of College Student Retention, 12*(2), 175–209. https://www.doi.org/10.2190/CS.12.2.d

Makridis, C., Piano, C. E., & DeAngelis, C. A. (2022). The effects of school closures on mental health: Evidence from the Covid-19 pandemic. *Social Science Research Network*. https://doi.org/10.2139/ssrn.4001953

Navarez, C., & Wood, J. L. (2010). *Community college leadership and administration: Theory, practice, and change*. Peter Lang.

Oakes, J., & Guiton, G. (1995). Matchmaking: The dynamics of high school tracking decisions. *American Educational Research Journal, 32*(2), 3–33. https://doi.org/10.2307/1163210

Peters, S. J., & Gentry, M. (2012). Group-specific norms and teacher-rating scales: Implications for underrepresentation. *Journal of Advanced Academics, 23*(2), 125–144. https://www.doi.org/10.1177/1932202X12438717

Ray, B. D. (2017). A systematic review of the empirical research on selected aspects of homeschooling as a school choice. *Journal of School Choice, 11*(4), 604–621. https://doi.org/10.1080/15582159.2017.1395638

Ray, B. D. (2023). *Research facts on homeschooling*. National Home Education Research Institute. Available at: https://www.nheri.org/research-facts-on-homeschooling/

Reis, S. M., Baum, S. M., & Burke, E. (2014). An operational definition of twice-exceptional learners: Implications and applications. *Gifted Child Quarterly, 58*(3), 217–230. https://doi.org/10.1177/0016986214534976

Renzulli, J. S. (1998). A rising tide lifts all ships. *Phi Delta Kappan, 80*(2), 104–111.

Robinson, A. (2012). Psychological science, talent development, and educational advocacy: Lost in translation? *Gifted Child Quarterly, 56*(4), 202–205. https://doi.org/10.1177/0016986212456077

Robinson, S. (2022). From the president's desk: #EndCCStigma: Social media as a tool to change public perception of 2-year colleges. *New Directions for Community Colleges, 2022,* 141–155. https://www.doi.org/10.1002/cc.20503

Roos, A. L., Bieg, M., Goetz, T., Frenzel, A. C., Taxer, J., & Zeidner, M. (2015). Experiencing more mathematics anxiety than expected? Contrasting trait and state anxiety in high achieving students. *High Ability Studies: The Journal of the European Council for High Ability, 26*(2), 245–258. https://doi.org/10.1080/13598139.2015.1095078

Selingo, J. (2020). *Who gets in and why: A year inside college admissions.* Scribner.

Subotnik, R. F., Olszewski-Kubilius, P., & Worrell, F. C. (2011). Rethinking giftedness and gifted education: A proposed direction forward based on psychological science. *Psychological Science in the Public Interest, 12*(1), 3–54. https://www.doi.org/10.1177/1529100611418056

Wood, S. (2023, October 9). Top colleges that still require test scores. *US News & World Report.* https://www.usnews.com/education/best-colleges/the-short-list-college/articles/top-colleges-that-still-require-test-scores

2

The History, Mission, and Context of the Community College

In Chapter 1, we made the case for why the community college could be a viable option for high achieving students. To be clear, we do not believe community colleges to be utopias, nor do we think four-year institutions are bad poor options. We do believe, however, that all prospective college students should have as much accurate and relevant information as possible in making big decisions such as where or whether to go to college. Today's higher education landscape in the U.S. is a cumulative history of its past. To fully understand community colleges of the twenty-first century, it is important to know their origin and their transformation.

The aim of this chapter is to provide readers with an overview of the community college's history, mission, and context. Each of these elements is crucial in understanding the contemporary community college landscape. We start with history, going all the way back to the year 1901 and mapping historical events to the growth and development of the community college. We then discuss the mission of the community college, which differentiates it from other postsecondary institutional types. Finally, we discuss the context of today's community colleges and situate these institutions among other types of postsecondary education institutions across the country.

DOI: 10.4324/9781003346210-2

History

Community colleges are a unique sector of higher education in the U.S. Joliet Junior College, touted as the first community college, was founded in 1901. Since their humble beginnings well over a century ago, these institutions have grown to over 900 community colleges spread across all the 50 states today (Kisker et al., 2023, p. 18). These institutions were born from the K-12 sector, and some of that history is still visible now. For example, staff positions such as college counselor persist, like a high school counselor. In the broader higher education space, however, these positions are usually separated into academic advisor, career development educator, and mental health counselor. Many early community colleges were first known as junior colleges and had a distinct emphasis on providing the first two years of a four-year, or bachelor's, degree. The idea was to take teaching pressure off the four-year sector, making space for more focus on the final two years of college along with research activity and the creation of new knowledge. However, four-year institutions never gave up the first two years.

Before going further, a brief history of higher education in the U.S. is necessary. The first colleges predate the inception of the country as independent and no longer under British rule. In 1636, as the 13 colonies were being created, what is now Harvard University was inaugurated. What followed was the establishment of the colonial colleges, nine institutions born before the American Revolution, which established the U.S. as a sovereign nation, independent of the British. These institutions, all of which started as private and religiously affiliated, include what are now Harvard University, the College of William and Mary, Yale University, Princeton University, Columbia University, the University of Pennsylvania, Brown University, Rutgers University, and Dartmouth College, the final colonial college, which was founded in 1769 (Lucas, 1994).

It was not until the mid- and late-1800s that institutions of higher education became more widespread across the U.S. The Morrill Land-Grant Acts of 1862 and 1890 catalyzed their expansion generally and the movement west. This federal legislation significantly impacted the growth of postsecondary education and marked a shift from the liberal arts to a more expansive curriculum including the agricultural and mechanical arts. This was also when the first Black colleges and universities and women's colleges and universities were created, marking expanded access to higher education (Lucas, 1994).

Heavily influenced by European models, between the years of approximately 1870 and 1920, the research university began to take shape in the U.S. (Menand et al., 2017). Notable examples include Johns Hopkins University and the University of Chicago. These institutions raised important questions about the purpose of higher education and whether and how differentiated institutional types could meet the needs of the nation and its people. As the research universities—with their focus on experimentation, scientific progress, and knowledge generation—began to take hold, so did the conversation regarding additional local, regional, and national higher education needs and ways to meet those needs. As mentioned above, the first community college, Joliet Junior College, was established in Illinois in 1901.

Some have argued that early junior colleges were meant to dissuade prospective students from entering higher education as a means of promoting social efficiency (Beach, 2011). In other words, community colleges did not necessarily begin with an open-access mission as is present today. The community college is often seen as democracy's college, the people's college, and an open door to higher education for all. However, much has changed since their original inception—including a massive growth spurt in the 1960s and 1970s when many new community colleges were created with a comprehensive focus and many existing junior colleges evolved into community colleges.

Interestingly, community colleges are one of the few educational innovations other nations across the world have sought to model. Some examples of countries that have implemented the two-year college option include Chile, Japan, Israel, France, Vietnam, Thailand, Zimbabwe, and India. (Raby & Valeau, 2009; Redden, 2010). On the other hand, U.S. community colleges have become an attractive destination for international students seeking an affordable on-ramp to a bachelor's degree or a specific sub-baccalaureate credential. Many community colleges have personnel, offices, and support readily available to support international students and institutional goals and initiatives meant to provide all students with a global perspective on their studies and future endeavors. Bunker Hill Community College in Massachusetts, for example, has a robust International Center, which has been in existence since 1995 (see https://www.bhcc.edu /internationalcenter/abouttheinternationalcenter/). More information on international student enrollment in U.S. community colleges can be found at: https://opendoorsdata.org/data/international-students/community-colleges-leading-institutions/.

U.S. history and the start and growth of the community college sector are intertwined. Educational institutions have long been charged with playing a role in solving society's problems. The community college is no exception. In the sections below, we will discuss various aspects of U.S. history, beginning with the start of the twentieth century and explain how these events are connected to the growth, expansion, and character of community colleges.

Early 1990s

At the start of the twentieth century, industry in the U.S. was expanding, and there was a need for trained workers to ensure the growth of an ever-strengthening economy. Industrial work was becoming more and more complex as efforts to improve efficiency became commonplace. The population was also growing. At the same time, there were pushes toward increased access to higher education. In the early 1900s, the colonial colleges, many of which are now private Ivy League institutions, such as Harvard University, Brown University, and the University of Pennsylvania, were well established, and the land-grant institutions, many of which are now public, such as Clemson University, the University of Connecticut, and the University of Idaho, were beginning to mature. Many land-grant institutions were initially involved in agricultural education but have since changed significantly. Many now offer a broad palette of science, technology, engineering, and math (STEM) degree programs. Principles of science were seen as key to societal progress at the turn of the

century, and colleges and universities were positioned to provide ongoing education and training within the sciences, among
other disciplines. Research was necessary to contribute to scientific knowledge, and institutions of higher education were seen
as engines of research, thus, resulting in new knowledge. The
advent of the two-year community college was recognized as a
way for four-year institutions to focus on upper-level teaching
and research activity.

Today, we see an ongoing expansion of participation in higher
education unthinkable in the early 1900s. Yet since the early
2000s, we have seen a national push in both college going and
college credential obtainment. This movement has been termed
The Completion Agenda (Baldwin, 2017) and has been supported
by various states, foundations, and the federal government.
This initiative was spurred on by the Great Recession of 2008
and continues today. Former President Barack Obama was the
movement's first champion in the White House. Increased college-going and credential completion among adults are seen by
some as one primary way to keep the U.S. competitive in the
global economy. Yet this movement is not without its critics, and
Isserles's (2021) work provides a brilliant critique. She noted that
sometimes student learning and development become secondary to completion, which might benefit institutions but is harm-
ful to students.

Agrarian to Industrial Society

As the nature of work in the U.S. has slowly shifted since the
early 1900s, society moved from a predominantly agrarian (a
focus on agriculture and farming) society to an increasingly
industrial one. There was a corresponding need for a formally
educated workforce. Institutions of higher education in the U.S.
have always tended to mirror the cadence of the nature of work,
the economy, and workforce needs. Most college students—
past, present, and future—understand that going to college and
obtaining a postsecondary credential have some bearing on
their future, often in work opportunities and potential earnings
from that work. Holding a postsecondary credential increases

lifetime earning potential. In fact, evidence from Georgetown University's Center on Education and the Workforce suggests that associate degree holders who are full-time workers will earn an average of $2 million across their lifetimes, while high school diploma holders will earn $1.4 million. See https://cew .georgetown.edu/cew-reports/collegepayoff2021/ for more information.

Work has never been more complex than it is today. We are living in an information age—an era of advanced manufacturing, robots, and artificial intelligence (AI). Manufacturing is more mechanized than ever before, food delivery robots are now common on college campuses, and many are experimenting with AI technologies through chat boxes, AI headshots, and self-driving cars. Technological advances are permeating nearly every aspect of modern work. There was a time when a high school graduate could easily move into a well-paying factory job, stay with a particular employer for their entire working life, and retire comfortably. That reality no longer exists. And the community college plays a major role—as it always has—in supporting workforce needs by preparing people to work and earn a livable wage within the current economy.

1930 to 1950

In 1930, 45 states were home to 440 junior colleges, which served around 70,000 students (Kisker et al., 2023, p. 16). The most significant growth was in the state of California, which currently serves 24% of all the nation's community college students. While this growth was significant, World War II marked the start of a major growth spurt within the community college sector across the nation.

World War II, which spanned from 1939 to 1945, changed the world and the course of civilization, perhaps more so than any other event in recorded history—aside from perhaps the advent of agriculture. As World War II ended, the U.S. federal government was eager to provide returning service members with opportunities to move back into and productively contribute to U.S. society. Therefore, the Servicemen's Readjustment Act of 1944 became federal law after the war. This original bill has long since expired, but the ongoing series of benefits afforded to veterans related to higher education and training, as a group, are referred to as the GI Bill. In the decades since 1944, the GI Bill has provided service members with ongoing access to higher education. The GI Bill framed going to college as an alternative to un(der)employment, and WWII veterans flooded into higher education.

World War II further accelerated the industrialization of U.S. society and opened the door to a globalized and interconnected world. To become and stay competitive in this newly emerging global economy, highly skilled prospective employees were needed. The community college continued evolving to meet this need. Upon their return from the war, these service members—in addition to going to college—also started families, building a large generation later termed *Baby Boomers*.

The Truman Commission

The 1947 report from the President's Commission on Higher Education, known as the Truman Commission, marked a moment in time when the federal government played a significant role in affecting higher education policy. Findings in the report also brought issues of higher education into public rhetoric. Two relevant recommendations of the report included: improving equity of and access to college going and expanding the role of community colleges. Expanding the role of the community college was seen as a pathway for expanding access to college. Much of what was recommended in the report was carried out in the decades following its publication.

The relationship between postsecondary education and government at the federal, state, and local levels has changed over time and remains in flux. Many institutions of higher education began as private and religiously affiliated entities—without significant governmental involvement. That said, federal, state, and local government involvement is a relatively new phenomenon. The Truman Commission marked an early and important connection between the federal government and the community college sector of U.S. higher education. Krendl Gilbert and Heller (2013) argued the report was "remarkably ahead of its time" and that "Commission members envisioned a higher education system, and by proxy a nation, radically more equitable, supportive, and open to social and intellectual advancement" (p. 439). Higher education, in large part because of community colleges, has never been more accessible in America than it is today.

1950 to 1970

Overseas, the Soviet Union successfully launched the first artificial Earth satellite in 1957 (also known as Sputnik). The fact that it was the Soviet Union (now known as Russia) and not the U.S. that accomplished this feat spurred on the Space Race. This race was centered on which country could push the envelope the farthest in terms of exploring outer space. Many attributed Sputnik's successful launch as the start of the science, technology, engineering, and math (STEM) emphasis in U.S. education, broadly, today.

Community colleges play an important and ever-expanding role in supporting STEM education at the postsecondary level. Through support from the National Science Foundation (NSF) and other entities, many community colleges are benefitting from external support for STEM education initiatives. One example is the Community College Innovation Challenge, which is supported by the American Association of Community Colleges and the NSF. Student teams participate in an Innovation Boot Camp and a competitive real-world solution design challenge. More information can be found at: https://www.aaccinnovationc hallenge.com/about-the-ccic/. Another example is the NSF's Enabling Partnerships to Increase Innovation Capacity (EPIIC) program, which supports community colleges, minority-serving institutions (MSIs), and predominantly undergraduate institutions (PUIs) build innovation ecosystems through partnerships. More information is available at: https://new.nsf.gov/funding/ opportunities/enabling-partnerships-increase-innovation -capacity.

Higher Education Act

The Higher Education Act of 1965 (HEA) was a significant catalyst for the growth and expansion of postsecondary education in the U.S. The HEA laid the groundwork for the federal grant and loan system in place today, which helps students access and afford higher education without having to rely (exclusively) on private loans. This also provided a clear schema regarding how public money would flow to higher education. States would provide appropriations to the public colleges, and the federal government would supply students with the grants and loans necessary to attend.

Since their humble beginnings, community colleges have been inequitably funded in comparison to their four-year institution counterparts (Mullin, 2010). Even though some community colleges benefit from local tax support, which sometimes stands in place of state-based support (Arizona is an example), they are still consistently asked to do more with less. State support for higher education has decreased over time. For example, in 1980, 60% of the nation's community colleges' public revenue came from state funding. In contrast, in 2020, only 34% of those revenues came from the state (Kisker et al., 2023). In the face of these funding challenges, however, community colleges remain resilient by focusing on providing a high-quality education for students while keeping costs low. Several new revenue streams have been pursued in recent decades such as mutually beneficial partnerships with business and industry, alumni development and fundraising, and entrepreneurial activity.

Upon the return of service members who served in World War II, birthrates in the U.S. began to increase. As a result, about 18 years after the end of the war, the Baby Boomer generation was graduating from high school and considering going to college. To account for this, many community colleges were established during the 1960s and 1970s. This was a huge growth period for community colleges in the U.S.

The community college sector has also endeavored to continuously expand its reach. For example, there are currently multiple generations in college right now, from Baby Boomers to Gen Z students. In addition, secondary students also now have access to the community college curriculum through dual and concurrent enrollment and credit opportunities, which will be the focus of Chapter 3. Finally, some community colleges are also offering baccalaureate degrees. This is a relatively new phenomenon and not widespread. Community colleges offer baccalaureate degrees in high-demand areas such as nursing and are not meant to compete with four-year institutions. Many community college baccalaureate degrees are applied, meaning the degree earned is focused on workplace applications of knowledge and skills. Florida is a national leader in this area, where many of the state colleges offer Bachelor of Applied Science (BAS) degrees.

1970 to 1980

Historically, higher education was accessible only to wealthy, White, Christian men. The college-going population has changed dramatically since Harvard was established in 1636. The Civil Rights Movement and the Women's Rights Movement in the 1960s and 1970s contributed to further opening the door to higher education. The Civil Rights Act of 1964 was a major civil rights and labor law that prohibited discrimination on the basis of race, color, religion, sex, and national origin. Title IX of the Educational Amendments of 1972, modeled on Title VI of the Civil Rights Act of 1964, forbade discrimination based on sex within educational programs supported by federal funding. While Title IX is perhaps most visible in the women's athletics space, its impact has been vast and wide. In 1972, the federal Pell Grant program was created to assist low-income students access higher education. Even though the buying power of the Pell Grant has decreased over time, this program further opened the gates of higher education to a broader segment of society.

1980 to 2000

In 1983, a report from the U.S. National Commission on Excellence in Education was published, entitled *A Nation at Risk: The Imperative for Educational Reform*. This report painted a bleak picture; K-12 schools were portrayed as failing, and their students were framed as underachieving academically (The

National Commission on Excellence in Education, 1983). This report was part of a surge in increased governmental oversight within educational entities, comparisons between nations regarding educational outcomes, and a direct connection between education and the economy. In addition, there was an increased emphasis on college as being an exclusively private versus a public good, which translated into less public financial support for higher education. These decreases have been consistently offset by increases in tuition and fees. If a college education was, in fact, a private good, then individuals were seen as being the ones to pay for it.

The Internet and Online Education

During the 1980s and 1990s, computers became more accessible to the general public. Many workplaces began the transition from strictly analog to increasingly digital operations. This was also a time when computers were increasingly present in people's homes. Once the Internet became public in 1993 (Grossman, 2023), online education was just a few years away. In the meantime, personal computing and its office-based affordances were becoming a part of the community college curriculum.

Once the Internet became more widely available, online higher education boomed in the late 1990s, and it is still booming, especially considering the COVID-19 pandemic. While it may seem counterintuitive, community colleges embraced the online course delivery movement. Seeking to meet the needs of nontraditional students who need flexible learning opportunities, community colleges have always been at the cutting edge of pedagogical advances, particularly those related to instructional technology. For-profit higher education giants offering sub-baccalaureate degrees and certificates, such as the Apollo Education Group, Inc., longtime owner of the University of Phoenix, exploded in the early days of online higher education, which gave and continues to give community colleges competition for online and non-traditional students. Many community colleges now have massive online course and program offerings. One example is Rio Salado College, part of Maricopa Community

Colleges, which is physically located in Tempe, Arizona. Today, some institutions have virtual *campuses*.

2000 to 2010

The first decade of the new millennium was full of critical events that have shaped the community college's recent history and led to increased campus safety measures at all institutions. To start, the terrorist attacks that took place on September 11, 2001 shook the nation. Homeland Security programs began to proliferate on college campuses, and the community college was no exception. The war that ensued further amplified the ongoing use of GI Bill benefits and the need for veteran support on college campuses. Additionally, social media took off during this time and has since changed the world. Students were connecting in new ways, and community colleges waded into the waters of social media marketing and communication. In 2007, the mass campus shooting at Virginia Tech brought issues of campus safety to the forefront of all college campus personnel, including the community college sector. Behavioral Intervention Teams (BITs) and campus crisis response protocols were put in place.

The Obama Presidency, Dr. Jill Biden, and the Great Recession

Barack Obama's presidency from 2009 to 2017 was pivotal in bringing the community college sector into the nation's consciousness. In addition, never before did we have a then Second Lady, Dr. Jill Biden, who also had a career teaching English and writing at a community college. As a community college faculty member, Dr. Biden helped bring the community college to the White House and to the attention of the American people. For example, in 2010, she hosted the first-ever White House Summit on Community Colleges (see https://obamawhitehouse .archives.gov/sites/default/files/uploads/community_college _summit_report.pdf). Furthermore, in 2015, President Obama proposed the America's College Promise initiative, inspired by the Tennessee Promise (see https://www.tn.gov/tnpromise .html). While not implemented, it was influential in shaping the many college promise programs we have today (see https://

obamawhitehouse.archives.gov/the-press-office/2015/01/09/
fact-sheet-white-house-unveils-america-s-college-promise-pro-
posal-tuition).

However, what really catalyzed these developments was the
2008 Great Recession and the community college being poised
as the nation's way out of the economic crisis. Community colleges experienced massive enrollment surges during this time.
This was also a time when policymakers began to focus attention
on the number of college graduates among the adult population.
The community college's access mission (i.e., open enrollment)
remained, but completion became the focus––and a driver of
state-level funding metrics.

2010 to Now

In October of 2015, the nation saw its first mass shooting at a community college. This tragic incident at Umpqua Community College
in Oregon was a tipping point in relation to community colleges
paying (more) attention to students' mental health. Since that time,
the literature on community college students' mental health has
grown, yet it pales in comparison to the research about students'
mental health within the four-year sector. In short, community college students have a higher prevalence of mental health concerns
and mental illness coupled with less access to resources than students at four-year institutions. The COVID-19 pandemic has had
further negative effects on college students' mental health overall.
At the same time, community colleges are now paying more attention to this issue than ever before and endeavoring to provide students or connect students with critical resources (Latz, 2023).

COVID-19 Global Pandemic

To be sure, the COVID-19 pandemic rocked all of higher education, and community colleges were no exception. Within a few
days and weeks in March of 2020, institutions of higher education across the U.S. shifted to online and virtual course delivery. Online conferencing platforms such as Zoom and Microsoft
Teams carried the day in terms of making computer-mediated
communication as humanized as possible. This shift laid bare

many obstacles students faced in continuing their postsecondary education journeys. Not all students had easy access to high-speed Internet. In fact, some students found themselves driving around town to locate free hotspots and doing their homework in parking lots of private businesses, such as fast food restaurants. Not surprisingly, student attrition at many community colleges increased during the pandemic for a myriad of non-academic reasons such as needing to work or provide childcare for younger siblings.

At present, community colleges are drawing upon their histories as resilient, agile, creative, responsive, open-access, affordable, and steadfast institutions of higher education. They are finding new ways to attract, enroll, and support students. They are helping business and industry bounce back from the pandemic shutdown, supply chain issues, and worker shortages in vital fields such as health care and teaching. And they continue to change lives for the better by providing their communities with high-quality educational opportunities of all kinds.

Values, Mission, and Vision

Now that we have provided a thorough history of the community college, we turn to a discussion on the values, mission, and vision of today's community colleges. Institutional values, and mission and vision statements offer a guide for those working within the institution and a window for those outside the institution. An institution's espoused values offer grounding as leaders navigate complex decision-making processes. The following mission-vision-inspired questions are often used by leaders as a litmus test: Does this decision represent an embodiment of our institutional values? Does this decision allow us to advance per our mission? Are these decisions moving us toward our vision going forward?

Relatedly, an institution's proclaimed values, mission, and vision allow outsiders a window into the organizational culture—at least to some degree. All this being said, examining institutional verbiage on these three elements is important. If an institution's values, mission, and vision are at odds with a student's personal values, mission, and vision, that institution may not be the best option for the student.

Let us examine the values, mission, and vision of Walla Walla Community College (WWCC), located in Walla Walla, Washington, as an example (https://www.wwcc.edu/about -wwcc/mission-and-vision/). First, the mission and vision statements are focused, clear, and concise. They provide a brief yet powerful snapshot of what the institution is all about. The institutional values, or guiding principles, are a list of key terms— including an explanation or definitions of those terms—that guide and ground institutional decision-making. WWCC has 10 guiding principles: learning opportunities, sense of community, diversity, health and humor, excellence, integrity, teamwork, innovation, personal and professional growth, and sustainability. Getting a sense of and gathering information about any given community college's values, mission, and vision are an important part of learning about that institution prior to admission.

Community colleges are characterized by their open-access admissions policies and affordable costs. They are seen as the people's colleges, democracy's colleges, and the gateway to higher education for all. In fact, many community colleges are Minority Serving Institutions (MSIs). Examples include Historically Black Colleges and Universities (HBCUs), Predominantly Black Institutions (PBIs), Hispanic-Serving Institutions (HSIs), Tribals Colleges and Universities (TCUs), and Asian American and Native American Pacific Islander-Serving Institutions (AANAPISIs). To learn more about MSIs, see https://cmsi.gse.rutgers.edu/. Open-access admissions means prospective students do not have to meet stringent requirements to be admitted to take courses. Minimum requirements typically include a high school diploma or GED. Standardized tests like the SAT or ACT are not required. Depending on how the specific institution defines college readiness, high school grade point average (GPA) and/or standardized test scores may be used for placement in either college-level or developmental courses. If a prospective student does not have these data points available, many community colleges use placement testing to determine at what level a new student should start coursework. Developmental courses, not typically offered for college credit, are meant to help students build the skills and knowledge necessary to be successful in college courses. Developmental coursework is typically delivered in the areas of reading, writing, and math. Sometimes community colleges also offer extended coursework tailored for students in pre-college and developmental coursework focused on study skills, time management, and campus resources.

Whereas many four-year institutions are known for their research activity, community colleges were started as teaching institutions and remain focused on student learning. This is not to say community college faculty are not scholars or that research is never a part of the sector. Research is just not the focus. And when community college faculty and personnel do engage in research, there is typically a teaching element where students are involved in the process. For example, undergraduate student research experience is considered a high impact practice that can help students discern whether certain fields or graduate education are of interest (AAC&U, 2023). In fact, many aspiring college faculty seek out the community college sector because of the teaching focus and lack of emphasis on or requirement of research.

Context

As explained above, community colleges are the most accessible institutions of higher education. Their admissions policies do not typically include the barriers found at other types of postsecondary institutions, such as mandating high school transcripts, English language fluency, minimum high school grade point averages, minimum scores on standardized tests, personal essays, involvement in extracurricular activities (sports, clubs, volunteer work), references, reference letters, or legacy admissions. No matter an individual's education background or literacy, ability, achievement, or skill level, an educational resource and college-going starting point are available at the community college. While not tied to college-level credit earning, many opportunities for educational advancement exist at the community college, such as GED preparation courses and adult basic education (ABE) opportunities, English language learning (ELL, also known as ESL or ESOL), and developmental education. These opportunities can be on-ramps to enrollment in credit-bearing college coursework that builds toward a college credential such as a certificate or degree.

Further, tuition and fees at community colleges are a mere fraction of the cost of most four-year institutions. That said, there is a cost associated with attending a community college. Even in geo-political areas (town, cities, counties, states) with promise programs like Kalamazoo, Michigan, or the state of Tennessee, where community college is free for those who qualify, there remain costs for some. These costs include the cost of not working while in class or studying, childcare, and transportation, for example. Community colleges enroll a significant proportion of students from low-income households. Many community college students are living in situational and generational poverty. In fact, a significant proportion of community college students have unmet basic needs, which include housing insecurity, food insecurity, and limited access to mental health resources (AACC, 2023; Kisker et al., 2023; Latz, 2023).

Summary

The community college is a living testament to its past. And its resiliency is a strong indicator of a bright future. While it is impossible to know what community colleges may look like over the next decades, what we do know is these agile institutions have never lost sight of their history and overall mission to serve diverse college students seeking to become more educated and productive citizens. In this chapter, we provided information about the history, mission, and context of community colleges in the U.S. Understanding each of these components is important to helping high achieving students understand all their postsecondary education options, of which the community college should be a part.

Discussion and Reflection Prompts

Support Prompts
   ◆ What did you find most interesting in reading about the history of the community college? How might you share some of this information with your students?

◆ Brainstorm a historical or current event not covered in this chapter. Then, trace that event to its relationship with higher education. What insights are you able to gain through this exercise?

◆ Visit the website of your local community college and search for the institution's history, values, mission, and vision. How do these compare with those highlighted in this chapter?

Student Prompts

◆ How much do you know about your local community college's history? How could you find out more? How might knowing more about its history impact what and how you think of the college?

◆ When thinking about where to attend college, what kinds of institutional values matter to you most?

◆ How important is attending college with a diverse student body to you? How can you find out information about an institution's student demography?

References

AAC&U (American Association of Colleges & Universities). (2023). *High-impact practices*. Available at: https://www.aacu.org/trending-topics/high-impact

AACC (American Association of Community Colleges). (2023). *Fast facts*. Available at: https://www.aacc.nche.edu/research-trends/fast-facts/

Baldwin, C. (2017). *The completion agenda in community colleges: What it is, why is matters, and where it's going*. Rowman & Littlefield.

Beach, J. M. (2011). *Gateway to opportunity? A history of the community college in the United States*. Stylus.

Grossman, D. (2023, May 16). When the Internet was invented, it was first just for scientists. *Popular Mechanics*. https://www.popularmechanics.com/culture/web/a43903714/when-was-internet-invented/

Isserles, R. G. (2021). *The costs of completion: Student success in community college*. Johns Hopkins University Press.

Kisker, C. B., Cohen, A. M., & Brawer, F. B. (2023). *The American community college* (7th ed.). Jossey-Bass.

Krendl Gilbert, C., & Heller, D. E. (2013). Access, equity, and community colleges: The Truman Commission and federal higher education policy from 1947 to 2011. *The Journal of Higher Education, 84*(3), 417–443. https://doi.org/10.1080/00221546.2013.11777295

Latz, A. O. (2023). *Community college student mental health: Faculty experiences and institutional actions.* Rowman & Littlefield.

Lucas, C. J. (1994). *American higher education: A history.* St. Martin's Griffin.

Menand, L., Reitter, P., & Wellmon, C. (Eds.). (2017). *The rise of the research university: A sourcebook.* University of Chicago Press.

Mullin, C. M, (2010, September). *Doing more with less: The inequitable funding of community colleges.* American Association of Community Colleges Policy Brief 2010-03PBL. Available at: https://files.eric.ed.gov/fulltext/ED522916.pdf

Raby, R. L., & Valeau, E. J. (Eds.). (2009). *Community college models: Globalization and higher education reform.* Springer.

Redden, E. (2010, June 15). The 'community college' internationally. *Inside HigherEd.* https://www.insidehighered.com/news/2010/06/16/community-college-internationally

The National Commission on Excellence in Education. (1983). *A nation at risk: The imperative for educational reform.* Available at: https://www.edreform.com/wp-content/uploads/2013/02/A_Nation_At_Risk_1983.pdf

3

College in High School Programs

Going to college requires strategic planning to minimize expenses and time to degree completion. Without good planning, students may take classes they do not need or miss out on opportunities to get a jump on college while still in high school, or even pre-high school. These opportunities are often offered at no or low cost to eligible students who are still in secondary education. Words of advice from others may include statements such as: *Take college courses now, it will save you money down the road!* Typically, a recommendation such as this means students should consider dual credit or Advanced Placement opportunities during their secondary education journey. Dual credit and Advanced Placement, the latter also referred to as AP, are two of the most common programs for high achieving high school students; however, in this chapter we want to make sure students are aware of *all* the options available to them. We also provide questions that we believe students might benefit from asking to determine the best fit programs that allow them to accelerate their college experience by taking college courses while still in high school. Many K-12 students participate in multiple programs that save them time and money in terms of college tuition and degree completion. In this chapter, we dive into early college credit access programs, especially college in high school (CiHS) opportunities, which we define very broadly, and provide important information on topics to consider when assessing college credit-bearing opportunities prior to graduating from high school.

DOI: 10.4324/9781003346210-3

About 88% of U.S. high schools offer some dual enrollment courses and around 34% of students graduate from high school with dual enrollment credit (Rhine, 2022). While national-level data are hard to access because of state-level nuances, these percentages are continuously growing as CiHS programs proliferate. CiHS is not only a way for students in secondary education to get ahead on college credits; it has also been shown to significantly improve student success in several important ways. Research has shown students who take a single dual enrollment course are more likely to graduate from high school on time, enroll in a four-year institution, successfully finish their first year of college, and successfully graduate with a bachelor's degree (Lee et al., 2022). This can be attributed to many factors, but two stand out. The first is *familiarity*. Students who take dual enrollment courses are exposed to college-level curriculum and expectations and, in cases where courses are taught at a higher education institution, the campus environment itself. This can help ease the transition from high school to college, which can be challenging for some students. The second factor is *confidence*. Students who can complete a dual enrollment course prove to themselves that they have what it takes to succeed at the collegiate level and the feeling of not being smart or capable enough is diminished (Allen & Dadgar, 2012).

Definitions

It is important to start with a discussion about various definitions of the different programs that allow high school (or younger) students to earn college credit through their local community college. The College in High School Alliance has a helpful glossary of terms (see https://collegeinhighschool.org/resources/glossary-of-terms/). Yet we provide some additional insights here. CiHS can have a variety of names. It is vital to understand the terminology used in your state and by your local schools and community colleges. Relatedly, it is also vital to know the specific definitions of those terms. It is common to hear a variety of terms such as dual credit, dual enrollment, concurrent enrollment, college in high school, or early college program. Other related phrases include honors classes, AP classes, and the International Baccalaureate.

Again, students should also be aware that various institutions of higher education may utilize unique names and terminology for their CiHS programs, which can differ from those used at other institutions or K-12 schools. Understanding these differences along with course and programmatic expectations will help students make sound decisions about their educational opportunities. In addition, it should be noted that both community colleges and four-year institutions participate in college in high school programs, and it is critical to know where any potential college credits are coming from and whether they are portable. For example, if a student amasses 15 credits from a community college while in high school, will those credits transfer into a four-year institution after high school graduation? It may take a bit of work to understand your options, but in the end, getting a jump on college is often a great decision for many students including high achieving and university-bound students.

Dual Credit, Dual Enrollment, and Concurrent Enrollment

The terms dual credit, dual enrollment, and concurrent enrollment are often used interchangeably. Yet they are usually defined slightly differently from one context to the next. It is vital to understand the local definitions of these terms. Dual credit is a term that generally means a student is earning credit at both the high school and college levels at the same time and within one course. In other words, one course *counts* for credit within both spaces. According to the College in High School Alliance (2021), the federal government suggests "a dual or concurrent enrollment program is offered by a partnership between at least one institution of higher education and at least one local educational agency through which a secondary school student who has not graduated from high school is able to enroll in one or more postsecondary courses and earn postsecondary credit that:

> (a) is transferable to the institution(s) of higher education in the partnership and (b) applies toward completion of a degree or recognized educational credential as described in the Higher Education Act of 1965.

> *(para. 8)*

Dual enrollment and concurrent enrollment are quite similar, although there are definitional nuances across contexts. The National Alliance of Concurrent Enrollment Partnerships (NACEP) is a source of information for this curricular configuration (see https://www.nacep.org/ for more information).

Honors and AP Courses

Taking honors courses in high school, if available, can be a strong way to prepare for the rigors of college courses and to bolster high school-level transcripts and grade point averages (GPAs), though these courses do not equate to college credit. Advanced Placement (AP) courses can lead to college credit; however, this is not automatic, and taking AP exams may involve fees. Students who take AP courses may subsequently decide to take the AP exam connected to that specific course. But this is not a requirement. These exams are offered through the College Board and administered inside high schools and at exam centers. More information can be found at: https://apstudents.collegeboard .org/. Earning a certain score on an AP exam can equate to earning college credit and/or testing out of some required or elective college courses.

Early College

Early college or early college high schools provide secondary students with the opportunity to earn an associate degree before graduating from high school. These programs usually commence in grade nine. Since the early 2000s, early college high schools have expanded and targeted specific socio-demographic groups such as students of color and students from low-income backgrounds. This expansion was in large part a result of the Bill & Melinda Gates Foundation's Early College High School Initiative, which has sought to invest in and expand access to secondary education success and postsecondary education access throughout the country. To learn more about early high school initiatives across the country, visit the Gates Foundation at: https://www.gates-foundation.org/ideas/media-center/press-releases/2004/12/strengthening-national-network-of-early-college-high-schools.

International Baccalaureate

Although it is a bit beyond the scope of this book, we want to mention the International Baccalaureate (IB). The International Baccalaureate Organization (IBO) offers an array of programs available for schools to offer their students. It should be noted, however, that the IB is not a bachelor's degree program, though it is a globally recognized series of educational programs. While there are reported to be more than 8000 IB programs offered worldwide, not every U.S. high school offers the IB curriculum. More specific and detailed information can be found through the IBO's website (see https://www.ibo.org/).

Partnerships and Implications

College in high school (CiHS) opportunities are typically offered to students following an agreement between a school or school district and a nearby community college or university. CiHS opportunities are typically opt in, meaning they are not automatic. Many schools or CiHS programs may have set regulations regarding who can participate. For example, in the state of Florida, CiHS agreements allow any public-school student from 6th to 12th grade with a 3.0 high school GPA and qualifying SAT, ACT, or Postsecondary Education Readiness Test (P.E.R.T.) scores access to CiHS. In this example, students are required to meet with their high school counselor, apply to the community college with a specific application, and then meet with an assigned Dual Enrollment Academic Advisor. While there may be additional steps for students to take, such as attending orientation or sending copies of their class schedules to their high school counselors, the critical piece is that all required steps are disclosed upfront by high school counselors and college representatives when a student applies to participate.

When pursuing CiHS opportunities, it is important for students to understand the implications of that decision. Once enrolled, students pursue college courses/credit in addition to attending high school. This can be challenging with long-lasting consequences, which need consideration. Students should explore, for example, whether the grades they earn in their dual credit courses are placed on both their high school and college transcript. It is important to note that in many cases once a student takes a dual enrollment course, for example, they will have an official college GPA. These credits do not *go away* when a student graduates from high school, and their college GPA will not reset when they start attending a community college or university full-time. As such, it is vital for students to know what they are signing up for because the results will have a lasting impact on their collegiate transcript—and beyond. In another example, many universities have a cap on the number of times students can retake a particular course, usually around three attempts. Some institutions will not allow students to repeat a course for which they earned a grade of C or higher. So, if a student takes a course through dual enrollment but wishes to take the course again at a college or university, perhaps to earn a higher grade, the dual enrollment course could impact whether they are approved to repeat the course. It is important that this kind of information is shared with students within any agreements or contracts they or their parents or guardians sign. Both students and their families should carefully review all documents, including and especially those requiring signatures, when registering for any CiHS program.

It is also important for students to understand that CiHS programs may be offered in a variety of modalities as well as in various locations. In other words, a student may need to travel to their local community college where the course is being offered on campus and taught by a college faculty member. Often, however, courses are offered at the student's high school and are taught by high school teachers whose credentials have been reviewed prior to being hired or contracted by the community college to teach the course. In some cases, college faculty travel to the high school to teach these courses. Finally, some courses are offered online, either synchronously or asynchronously. Synchronous online courses require students to be present online at a particular day and time to attend virtual courses with other students and the instructor on platforms such as Zoom. Asynchronous courses allow students the flexibility to work on the material when they can, although assignments will have due dates and times. When taking asynchronous courses, students must have excellent time management and study habits where they create a self-imposed structure. This often means setting aside specific days/times to complete readings, watch/listen to lectures, and/or engage in homework independently.

When deciding to participate in CiHS programs, it is also important to consider the student's personal and extracurricular activities. As mentioned above, effective time management is always key to academic success, so understanding and planning for all other commitments are important. Dual enrollment courses may not always fall within the typical 8 a.m. to 3 p.m. school day. In addition, some students will not have taken fully asynchronous online courses before, so any dual credit course offered in this modality should be considered prior to enrollment. In sum, it is important to be aware of what skills students will need to possess to be successful in CiHS. Effective time management, self-motivation, and organizational skills are just a few skills students will need to be successful in CiHS programs.

FERPA: Family Educational Rights and Privacy Act

Once a student enrolls in a CiHS, regardless of their age, they will be bound by some of the same policies and procedures as other college students. For example, when enrolled in dual enrollment programs, students are protected under the federal Family Educational Rights and Privacy Act, commonly known as FERPA. This federal law provides parents/guardians with certain (but limited) rights to their child's educational records within the K-12 system; however, it is important to note the following:

> If a student is attending a postsecondary institution—at any age—the rights under FERPA have transferred to the student. However, in a situation where a student is enrolled in both a high school and a postsecondary institution, the two schools may exchange information on that student.
>
> (U.S. Department of Education, n.d.,
> para. 1)

If the student is under 18, the parents still retain the rights under FERPA at the high school and may inspect and review any records sent by the postsecondary institution to the high school.
(U.S. Department of Education, n.d.,
para. 1)

Additionally, the postsecondary institution may disclose person-ally identifiable information from the student's education records to the parents, without the consent of the eligible student, if the student is a dependent for tax purposes under the IRS rules.
(U.S. Department of Education, n.d.,
para. 1)

For those dually enrolled, this means the students become respon-sible for their educational information and procedures. As a *col-lege* advisor, one of the most common, yet difficult, situations arise when a parent calls on behalf of their student to inquire about courses, grades, registration, or other matters related to their stu-dent's experience with the community college. In these instances, college staff and faculty must adhere to FERPA regulations, which limits what information they are able to share with parents or guardians. Yet not all institutions of higher education will inter-pret federal (or other) mandates in the exact same way. It is cru-cial for students to understand that in many cases, they will be fully responsible for how they engage with the community college and that they must be the ones, not their parents or guardians, to email, call or discuss their dual enrollment experience with col-lege staff or faculty.

It is also important to note that if there are concerns related to the CiHS program in relation to the student's high school experi-ence or outcome, parents can meet and discuss the student's edu-cational information with the high school representatives, such as high school counselors, college and career readiness coordi-nators, teachers, and administrators, but not always the college without a student's express approval. Additional information regarding FERPA may be found at studentprivacy.ed.gov.

Advanced Placement

Because Advanced Placement (AP) is another common program among high achieving students that helps students get a jump on college, here we provide some additional information on the potential option. AP courses are established by the College Board and largely standardized across the country. AP courses are taught in many K-12 systems and commonly offered during the late middle school and high school years. Students who are homeschooled or attending a school that does not offer AP courses may be able to enroll in AP courses offered elsewhere.

Most schools have requirements in place for students to be able to participate in AP level courses, such as taking and doing well in a prerequisite course or taking a placement test to show readiness for the advanced coursework. It is important that students speak with their assigned high school counselor to understand the requirements and to ensure taking AP courses is in their best interest. AP courses are taught by high school teachers, and students earn high school credit for the courses. Additionally, students may also take the standardized AP exam, which is available after they pass the course. Depending on their total score on the AP exam, students may be able to earn college credit in addition to high school credit. It is possible for students to take AP courses and not take the standardized exam at the end of the course if they do not wish to earn college credit. So, in this example, the student would earn high school credit for the AP course but not college credit. One barrier that can affect whether students sit for the AP exam is the associated cost. Students are encouraged to speak with their counselors should they be unable to pay for the cost of an AP exam as there may be assistance available to help families with the expense.

Advanced Placement tests are scored on a scale of 1–5, where 5 is the highest score. A score of 3 will earn a passing grade and, in most cases, some college credit, though this can vary by course and transfer institution. College transfer credit is always determined by a student's receiving institution. In other words, how institutions apply AP credit can vary. Some colleges may transfer AP credit in as general electives, while others may award the credit to program-specific requirements. Many institutions have an equivalency chart that students can review that lets them know how their credits could be applied. Here is an example from Elkins Community College: https://elgin.edu/admissions/testing-services/advanced-testing/ap-charts/. Unlike dual credit courses, however, AP grades are not automatically applied to a college transcript. This means students will need to request their College Board score report be sent to their desired institution(s). Students who take AP courses have a great deal of flexibility and can choose whether they wish to have AP credit transferred to a college or not. It is also important to note that while students may earn college credit hours through AP, their college GPA will not be impacted by the credit. No GPA is associated with the AP credits, so some students may choose this option over other CiHS options. Students should understand which AP exam scores will be needed to earn college credit and how those credits will transfer not only to a student's chosen college but also to their program of study.

Many course options are available through College Board. Currently, over 35 AP courses are available in the areas of Art, English, History and Social Sciences, Math and Computer Science, Sciences, and World Languages and Culture (see https://apstudents.collegeboard.org/course-index-page). However, not every high school offers AP courses, and even if they do, they may not offer very many. To reiterate, it is crucial that students have consistent communication with their high school counselor to best plan their educational path and take advantage of such opportunities. These options can help high school students save money and time. Finally, additional information regarding AP courses and exam fees can be found on the College Board website at www.collegeboard.org.

Costs

While some CiHS programs are free for students, not all are. As such, students and their families need to do their homework and ask questions so they are not surprised by fees for college courses and/or AP tests. Regular contact and communication with school counselors and college readiness coaches (if available) are necessary. Answers needed to make an informed decision and one that works for students and families are available, but curiosity and proactivity are necessary.

Advanced Placement, as explained earlier, is standardized across the country though not every high school offers AP courses. As of 2024, for students studying in the U.S. and taking the exam at their designated school, the cost of the exam will be $98 (see https://apstudents.collegeboard.org/exam -policies-guidelines/exam-fees). There could be additional fees tacked on by the school to cover test proctoring or administrative costs. The College Board does have a policy for fee reductions if an individual has significant financial need. Eligible students can reduce each AP exam by $36. According to the College Board, additional support through various state funding sources may be available, and students are encouraged to contact their designated AP school counselor for assistance. In addition to the cost of AP exams, it is important to note that students will be able to send one free score report every year an AP exam is taken to their desired college, university, or scholarship organization (see https://apstudents.collegeboard .org/sending-scores/free-score-send). A fee will be charged if additional score reports are needed. All reports must be requested and paid for by the student via an online account with the College Board.

Costs can vary drastically from state to state. Some states have more than one type of CiHS program, and each program can potentially have different costs and different rules on who covers those costs. The 50-State Comparison: Dual/Concurrent Enrollment Policies report by the Education Commission of the States offers a comprehensive list of dual enrollment programs and policies across the country (see https://www.ecs .org/50-state-comparison-dual-concurrent-enrollment-poli-cies/). Resources included in the report are based on state policies from a variety of sources. We suggest visiting the *Finance* section of this report to review how CiHS programs are defined and funded in specific states. Individuals can filter by their state and see what the CiHS programs are called in their area, the description of the student costs, and the source of where the information was found. This comparison tool is critical for families as CiHS programs can vary not only from state to state but also from school to school. Public school, private school, and home school students may have different requirements, criteria, and potential costs. Lastly, it should be noted that additional costs in the form of transportation or course materials may be incurred.

Making Choices

Many factors go into the decision to participate in CiHS programs. It is important to start with the end goal in mind and to do research to best understand options and next steps. While this may look different for every student, there are a few simple questions that may be helpful throughout the decision-making process:

◆ Which career paths are students most interested in?
◆ Which colleges are at the top of students' application lists, and (how) do those schools accept CiHS program credits and/or AP courses?
◆ Which major might students wish to pursue in college?
◆ Will students be attending a community college or four-year institution after graduating from high school?
◆ Does the student's high school offer CiHS programs and/or AP courses? If so, what are the details of those opportunities? If not, what alternatives might be available?
◆ What are the fees and overall costs of the options, and can the student/family afford the expenses? If not, what resources, scholarships, or support might be available?

Once students answer—or at least consider—these questions, they should have a good start for further reflection and eventual decision-making.

Career Paths

Certain career paths have unique college-level course requirements. Many pathways are *friendly* to CiHS credits, especially
career paths that require a bachelor's degree. Professional pathways can often be more selective in terms of transferring in
earned credit. For example, if a student plans to attend medical school, they will want to understand the implication of taking dual enrollment and/or AP science courses. Medical school
applications are extremely competitive and largely based on the
GPA earned in students' science courses. There may also be some
consideration regarding where those science courses were taken.
As stated earlier, AP courses do not impact a student's GPA. That
said, a student may be better served taking college-level science
courses during high school and earning high grades, rather than
taking AP coursework in high school. Dual enrollment courses
result in a letter grade, but if a student takes an entry-level college
course during high school, such as Introduction to Chemistry,
they need to be aware that they may be placed in a significantly
higher-level science course during their first year of college, such
as Biochemistry. By earning the college credit in high school, they
have, in essence, completed the prerequisite for the higher-level
course and will be placed as such, which may affect their grade
in the higher-level course and their GPA. If a student is interested
in highly competitive programs such as medicine or engineering, they should reach out to a college academic advisor to discuss whether participating in dual enrollment and/or taking AP
courses is a good strategy while still in high school. If a student
is advised against taking dual enrollment and/or AP courses in
a particular discipline, this does not mean they cannot enroll in
any AP or dual credit courses. In the medical school example
above, the student may be advised against taking dual enrollment or AP science courses yet encouraged to enroll in English
or Humanities dual credit or AP courses. Again, it is always recommended to seek guidance from an advisor.

Credit Transfer

Students transferring courses to a college or university may lose some portion of the credits they attempt to transfer. That may seem shocking, but it is an unfortunate reality. In short, not all college credits are portable. This loss can be a result of credit mismatch, or students simply taking the wrong course(s) for their degree. For example, a student may take a dual credit English Composition course in high school only to find out it does not align with English courses at their receiving college or university. In other words, the courses may not be an apples-to-apples comparison in terms of course descriptions or learning outcomes. In some cases, credit earned through dual enrollment may be transferable as elective credits instead of a required course. When deciding which CiHS program courses to take, it is important to look for a Transfer Credit Equivalency Guide at the college a student plans to attend. An example of such a planning tool can be found at: https://assist.org/. If there is not an online guide at their transfer institution, students should contact the institution directly, usually the Registrar's Office, to obtain information on the transferability of dual credit, dual enrollment, and/or concurrent enrollment courses.

College Experience

Another factor to consider prior to making decisions about CiHS or AP coursework is what kind of college experience students seek. If a student graduates from high school with an associate degree, then matriculates into a four-year institution as a third-year student at age 18, it can be a jarring transition and challenging overall postsecondary experience. Accumulating a great deal of college credit before completing high school accelerates college completion—both at the associate and bachelor's level—so much so that the college experience changes dramatically. If a student earns an associate degree while still in high school, that means the first half of their four-year college experience will be quite different than the second half. Alternatively, if a student takes only one or two dual enrollment courses in high school, they will spend more time in college and have a more traditional college experience yet pay more for a college education. Some might argue there are benefits to this latter approach. First, taking fewer college classes while in high school gives students more time to develop and narrow down which career path and academic major they would like to pursue—at least initially. About one-third of all college students change their major at least once (National Center for Educational Statistics, 2017), which means students who change majors after they have completed the bulk of their general education courses in high school may be faced with some credit mismatch. In this case, it is likely the student will need to take additional courses that suit the new major. Second, it is important to remember that college is more than just taking classes. In college, students will have the opportunity to join clubs, engage with professional organizations, participate in study abroad, complete internships, and make connections with a variety of other people. These types of experiences not only help students develop life skills and career competencies; they are also valuable in terms of social-emotional development. Entering college with minimal college credit gives students more time to experience all those possibilities now available to them in college. Students and their families should consider the college experience writ large and consider how an accelerated approach to earning college credit while in high school might impact the student overall.

Special Programs and Opportunities

Another factor students should consider when accelerating college completion while in high school is the impact it could have on their acceptance into some special programs at the community college. For example, some honors programs—often very appealing to high achieving high school students—may have a limited curriculum because of their transfer articulations and guaranteed admissions agreements with four-year institutions. In other words, these programs may not have many or any honors courses to offer a student who has amassed a great deal of credit while in high school. Some of these honors transfer agreements provide full scholarships to four-year institutions; thus, a student's inability to be accepted into an honors program because of the number of college credits they earned prior to college could be an unfortunate consequence of earning early college credits. For some students, this might result in a loss of scholarship dollars as well. This serves as another reminder for students to research all angles of CiHS programs, as there could be both intended as well as unintended consequences. Additional information about honors programs at the community college can be found in Chapter 5.

Summary

In this chapter, we outlined the contours of pursuing college credit while still in secondary education. We discussed and defined a variety of terms and underscored the complexity of this topic. There is much to consider when making decisions about CiHS programs. Gathering information, asking questions, and intentional planning are vital. There is no correct answer or definite pathway for high achieving students when it comes to pursuing college credits while still on the secondary school journey. At the same time and to the extent possible, all avenues should be interrogated and fully understood.

Discussion and Reflection Prompts

Support Prompts

♦ What opportunities for earning college credit while in high school are available to your students?

♦ Which students tend to benefit from these programs? Are there ways to make these opportunities more equitable and accessible?

♦ How do students make decisions about participating in available CiHS programs? Do students and families have all the information they need to make sound decisions?

Student Prompts

- ♦ How much do you know about your school's CiHS programs? How might you learn more?
- ♦ What are your post-high school intentions? What kinds of college experiences do you want to have? Are you interested in graduate school? What is your ideal first job or career? How might the answers to these questions affect whether and/or how you participate in CiHS programs?

References

Allen, D., & Dadgar, M. (2012). Does dual enrollment increase students' success in college? Evidence from a quasi-experimental analysis of dual enrollment in New York City. *New Directions for Higher Education, 2012*(158), 11–19.

College in High School Alliance. (2021, December 14). *Glossary of terms*. https://collegeinhighschool.org/resources/glossary-of-terms/

Lee, J., Fernandez, F., Ro, H. K., & Suh, H. (2022). Does dual enrollment influence high school graduation, college enrollment, choice, and persistence? *Research in Higher Education, 63*(5), 825–848.

National Center for Education Statistics. (2017, December). *Data point: Beginning college students who change their majors within 3 years of enrollment*. U.S. Department of Education. Available at: https://nces.ed.gov/pubs2018/2018434/index.asp

Rhine, L. (2022, September 1). The power of dual enrollment: The equitable expansion of college access and success. Blog. The U.S. Department of Education. Available at: https://blog.ed.gov/2022/09/the-power-of-dual-enrollment-the-equitable-expansion-of-college-access-and-success/

U.S. Department of Education. (n.d.). *Protecting student privacy*. Available at: https://studentprivacy.ed.gov/faq/if-student-under-18-enrolled-both-high-school-and-local-college-do-parents-have-right-inspect

4

Workforce Education and Development

The community college is a great place for high school students to begin their career exploration, but this can be a scary time for many students as they start their higher education journey. There are so many options to consider that students may not know where to start. Consider when you were asked, *So, what do you want to do with your life?* or *What do you want to be when you grow up?* These are hard-to-answer questions that people get asked as young as 5 years old. Fast forward to the age of 17 or 18 and starting the fall semester of your senior year in high school. Do you know the answer to such questions even now? Most 18-year-olds do not know what they want to do for a living, let alone what they need to prepare for a career. Furthermore, what they end up doing for a living will likely be many different things. Employment opportunities change rapidly, and employees need various and ever-evolving skill sets and knowledge bases to realize long-term success. Young people must start to develop career readiness at some point. And while this may seem like too much to consider at a young age, take heart—the community college might be the perfect place to start.

Many high school graduates can celebrate that they have taken a great first step by attending one of the nation's community colleges. Unlike a four-year experience, the community college can offer an educational opportunity that is more personal,

DOI: 10.4324/9781003346210-4

less expensive, and more flexible to meet students' needs. High achieving graduates have gained math and language skills in high school, maybe through AP or dual credit courses, that give them a jump on completing required general education classes in college. They may enroll in the community college with a longer-term plan, which includes transfer to a four-year institution. The flexibility of community college courses allows students to take up a part-time job at a local employer to gain critical skills they may need in preparation for their baccalaureate degree and field of work. Many students need to work, including traditional-aged students; hence, a residential college experience with tra-ditional course scheduling—interspersed during the weekday and in-person—may not the best solution for them. Community colleges tailor their course modalities and schedules for every type of student, including those who have to work while in col-lege. While transfer pathways and associate degrees are often the focus of community college students, other students may seek short-term credentials and workforce training. Whatever the students' goals and interests are, community college career centers can help learners get off to a good start. Often, after stu-dents meet with their community college academic advisors and career coaches, they become more comfortable with their chosen pathway and decision to attend community college. Community college advisors make the time to identify how they can assist students in finding their best-fit pathways to transfer or enter the workforce. As an incoming student's plan is taking shape, they become excited to see what the future holds. Many students prefer and perform better in intimate one-on-one classroom set-tings. Community college students offer diverse opportunities and experiences, which can boost student success.

The focus on transfer opportunities and workforce develop-ment in the community college can be the key foundation to students' success. This chapter is focused on workforce educa-tion and development at the community college. Workforce edu-cation and development may also be referred to as vocational education, technical education, or career and technical educa-tion—and this is *not* an exhaustive list. Community colleges offer credit and non-credit programs, certifications, licensures, and diplomas that help students bridge from their academic programs into the workforce within the local community. These programs are often supported by business and industry partners and impact and improve the community's economic system while supporting and retaining a high-quality workforce in the local area. As students consider attending a community college, it is important they recognize the plethora of different avenues available to them. These paths can lead to the success students seek in their career. There are many postsecondary education pathways beyond earning a four-year degree, and community colleges are at the forefront of offering these options.

Career Education

High school counselors and career and college readiness professionals can certainly offer students information and guidance on postsecondary options, though we suggest students seek out as much guidance and support as possible in this area. Prospective students have many resources available to them through the local community college. One of these resources is the office dedicated to providing career education. Meeting with a career educator can be an important step in fully understanding how to pursue a workforce-focused credential. Furthermore, incoming community college students may struggle to understand why meeting with a career coach is helpful if they have plans to transfer to a four-year institution. Students should recognize that the career coach may spend most of the first session understanding who the students are as people and what interests them. These student-career coach interactions help students understand and navigate not only their next steps in higher education but also in work and life. Students, whether bound for transfer or employment, may be handed a resume template and asked to complete it by a specific date so the career coach can give valuable feedback. After getting to know the student holistically, the career coach may set up action items to prepare the student for their next steps and schedule a follow-up session. Some career coaches offer bi-weekly meetings to assist students in preparing for, as an example, their first job interview. After meeting with a career coach who spent the time to understand what the student enjoyed, assisted with establishing long-term goals, helped build their resume, and prepared them for a possible internship or job interview, the student often realizes that they would have benefited from meeting a career coach sooner. Some students are even shocked to discover that they may not need to transfer to a four-year institution to work in their desired field. The career coach may be able to help define and refine a pathway enabling the student to enter the workforce within a short period of time.

Workforce Education and Development

Workforce education and development are a significant component of the community college mission. Community colleges help prepare employees to take up jobs in their communities. Many students benefit from community colleges' specialized training and micro-degree options. It is important to note that some workforce education and development programs are offered as non-credit options. Relatedly, the costs associated with these non-credit-bearing options tend to operate outside of the tuition and fee schedule connected to credit-bearing pursuits. Students must take all this into consideration.

Many high schools focus on educating students seeking a college degree and assist them in exploring the available academic programs. However, some students feel already prepared to join the workforce or are adult learners already invested in an industry but would like to continue their education. The community college option is very appealing for those wanting to get into the workforce faster with fewer financial obligations and less college debt attached. Vocational training has become a higher priority in the U.S. because it improves job quality and the overall economic health of local communities. Vocational education and training (VET) programs, another phrase used to indicate workforce education and development, are critical markers of success in transitioning employees into the workforce (Myers & Kellogg, 2022). VET programs, many of which are offered at the community college, help students gain skills for various industries so they are *work-ready*. Many states coordinate, oversee, and provide workforce prepared-ness programs where students can take specific classes and earn certifications to be adequately trained for their career path. Community colleges are partnering with businesses and industries in their local region to help become leaders in and destinations of choice for workforce development. These mapped-out career pathways have helped students feel more confident committing their time to community college edu-cation with strong prospects for employment after credential completion. For some students, workforce readiness starts as early as high school, where high schools are preparing "three sequential courses ... aligned to regional college programs that include intensive work-based learning experiences" (Myers & Kellogg, 2022, p. 37). States with curricula aligned with work-force competencies in high-demand areas, such as nursing, and clear connections across the educational continuum to the local communities' workforce, have a higher chance of retaining a quality workforce in their region.

Partnerships with Business and Industry

The ongoing increase in the number of community college part-nerships with business and industry has been a critical com-ponent of community colleges focusing on their capacity to support and educate the local workforce. These partnerships have helped community colleges located in close proximity to business develop a shared mission, vision, and goals, creating an infrastructure for strong leadership within the educational and local community systems because of the increased collab-orative efforts. Local businesses are investing their energy and time in the nearby community colleges to help prepare high-quality entry-level professionals who are work-ready and often prepared through internships. Credentials offered through com-munity colleges have currency. In fact, local employers actively seek employees who have these credentials. Graduating from a community college can often lead to more development opportu-nities where employers want to retain strong talent. The stream of community college-prepared new employees helps local com-panies continue investing resources in the community college, where they will enhance existing workers' skills through various continuing education programming.

One major mission of the community college is to supply a trained workforce to local economies. They accomplish this goal through various programming options, including accelerated programs, condensed semesters, specific trade certifications, specialized certificates, or two-year associate degrees that can stack into bachelor's degrees. Community colleges offer much more than just two-year degrees. For example, many students benefit from community colleges' specialized training and micro-degree options.

Condensed Semesters

Many community colleges operate on a standard 16-week semester, while others have moved to a condensed semester time frame. Eight-week semesters and increased innovation and flexibility regarding developmental coursework have helped community colleges improve student completion rates, an important metric where community colleges have historically struggled. There is evidence that shorter eight-week semesters may provide a more equitable solution for community college students, as it allows them to focus on fewer courses at a time and helps them re-enter the program more quickly if they have to drop out (Ruf, 2021). Some institutions began this transition to shorter semesters during the COVID-19 pandemic (see more on this in Chapter 8). However, as they saw benefits to their students, many two-year institutions decided to continue with the shorter semester timelines. For example, Trident Technical College in South Carolina saw an improvement in graduation, student persistence, and course completion rates within the first five years of implementation (Ruf, 2021). Students may be willing to change from part-time to full-time college attendance with the shortened eight-week semester, as they only need to take two courses at a time to complete four courses within the traditional 16-week semester period. Many older and working community college students like this shortened class load because they often have significant work and family responsibilities outside of the classroom. Additionally, some students feel less overwhelmed making the eight-week commitment (Ruf, 2021). It is essential to consider what works for any given student before enrolling in a long-term versus a short-term semester. Some institutions offer the same courses in a variety of semester or term lengths and modalities. Students should understand how they learn best and how their class experiences will unfold ahead of time.

Accelerated Programs

Another option at some community colleges is accelerated degree programs which, for some high achieving students, meet their desire to graduate quickly. Time is especially precious for non-traditional students who juggle work and family obligations and for those eager to transfer to their four-year institution. Such a rapid pace to completion is not for every student, however, so it is important to know how a student learns best. College without success is not a good outcome for any student. Accelerated Study in Associate Programs (ASAP) helps students achieve degrees and certificates in highly condensed time frames. Sometimes, these programs come with financial assistance and significant institutional resources. For example, the City University of New York's (CUNY) two-year college system offers ASAP and provides students eligible for financial aid with "a tuition and fee gap scholarship, so there is no cost to attend college" (CUNY, n.d., para. 1). In addition, CUNY also offers Accelerate, Complete, and Engage (ACE), a total student support structure, which includes academic advice, career education, textbook access, and transportation support (see https://www1.cuny.edu/sites/asap/about/asap-at-a-glance/). In Indiana, Ivy Tech Community College also offers ASAP, which assists students with earning an associate degree in just 11 months. Students take courses across five eight-week terms, and attend classes Monday to Friday, from 9 o'clock in the morning to 5 o'clock in the evening (see https://www.ivytech.edu/programs/special-programs-for-students/accelerated-programs/accelerated-associate-degree-asap/). Washtenaw Community College in Ann Arbor, Michigan, offers a variety of accelerated business-related certificate programs such as Supply Chain Essentials and Business Enterprise Basics (see https://www.wccnet.edu/learn/accelerated.php for details).

Again, an accelerated program such as ASAP is not a fit for every community college student, but for many it is just the right balance of rigor and a shortened time to completion. Many students thrive in accelerated formats, while others benefit from a traditional 16-week semester. Students must discuss these options with school counselors, academic advisors, and others to find the best fit for their learning preferences and other life obligations.

Types of Credentials

Micro-Credentials and Digital Badges
With micro-credentials gaining popularity among learners and employers, who better to offer them than your local community college? Earning a micro-credential is only part of the unique offerings of community colleges. The smaller student-to-staff ratios often mean community colleges can offer other specialized services to help students transition from high school to their career choice. These short-term learning programs focus on specific skills or learning objectives. Microdegrees, or micro-credentials, are good options for students still determining their major as they allow learners to dive into coursework. Additionally, students can enhance their resumes and job competencies quickly without the cost of (and time to complete) a full degree.

Opportunities to earn micro-credentials differ from institution to institution. Sometimes, these opportunities are completely free for enrolled students—as well as faculty and staff at the institution. An example of this can be found at Austin Community College (see https://sites.austincc.edu/digital -fluency/microcredentials/), in Texas. In this example, current students can earn a variety of micro-credentials such as Word Processing, Data Management, and Interactive Media. While these micro-credentials are non-credit, there are pathways that will cross walk them to credit. Furthermore, earning a micro-credential typically comes with a portable digital badge, which can be showcased on a resume and work-related media such as LinkedIn.

The Community College of Aurora (CCA) in Colorado offers a number of micro-credentials in behavioral health (see https://

ccaurora.edu/news-press/campus-happenings/kick-start-your
-career-with-a-micro-credential-in-behavioral-health/). Often,
these micro-credentials are created to address a local or regional
workforce need. They are created in close partnership with
employers who have identified a high-need area in their operations. This was the case with CCA, as these micro-credential
offerings grew from an unmet demand for qualified mental
health professionals in the area (Brownlee, 2023).

Certificates

Community colleges offer students opportunities to explore
unique and specialized career paths through certificate programs without them having to make significant time or financial
commitments. Community college certificate programs are relatively short, lasting anywhere from a few months to a year. This
results in less overall tuition and/or fee costs, and the completion
rates for certificate programs are often higher than in associate
degree programs. The number of courses, amount of time, and
credit requirements for certificates are generally less than those
required for an associate degree but more than a micro-credential. Many certificate programs can be completed within one year
and are focused on a specific skill set. Generally, students do not
need to pass a proficiency test as required by licensure, but they
must complete their courses with passing grades. Like micro-
credentials, certificates can also be stacked into other credentials
that eventually can lead to completion of an associate degree or
even a bachelor's degree.

Specialty Certificates

The variety and creativity of community college certificates are
often surprising, with most institutions offering programs that
represent the needs of their local communities and job markets.
Some colleges have begun reviewing their program outcomes
to substantiate the effectiveness of the credential for student
economic outcomes. For example, in 2011, Texas State Technical
College's state funding was linked to the income increases students receive as an outcome of the credential. As a result of this

policy and subsequent review, several programs were canceled because of inefficiencies, while others continued to grow. On the bright side, the graduating students' income increased by 140%, according to Michael Reeser, the college's chancellor (Burke, 2022). Just as associate degree program outcomes must demonstrate their value to students and advisory boards to remain viable, so too must other college credentials. Because of this scrutiny, community colleges are working hard to align their curriculum and programs with the economic needs of the communities.

Finger Lakes Community College in upstate New York's wine region is one of several community colleges that offers students the chance to learn the skill of winemaking by earning a Viticulture Certificate (see https://www.flcc.edu/viticulture-center/). This Viticulture Certificate helps students obtain entry-level positions in vineyard management, winery operations, and wine center management. Furthermore, Finger Lakes Community College also offers an Associate of Applied Science degree in Viticulture and Wine Technology for students who wish to expand their education. Other community colleges in areas such as the state of Washington and Northern Michigan also offer Viticulture Certificates and associate degrees. These geographical areas are rich with regional wineries and vineyards, making this specialized educational opportunity a significant inroad to exciting career paths. In this way, community college workforce-focused certificate programs align with the industries located in their communities.

Considering the prominence of the hospitality industry in the U.S., culinary programs can be found at many community colleges across the country. Students passionate about food science, for example, can earn a certificate in Culinary Arts from Bucks County Community College in Pennsylvania (see https://www.bucks.edu/catalog/majors/business/pastry/). This certificate will help students access entry-level positions such as chefs, cooks, bakers, or other hospitality positions. Often, students need clarification on a career path and are hesitant to over-invest in the educational process. A certificate in culinary arts is a great way to gain knowledge and experience, make local connections, and, in essence, try a career on for size. Like other certificate programs, students may stack their short-term credentials into an associate degree should they wish to continue their college education. It is vital that students understand transfer and continuing education agreements and policies early in their college career.

Many students seek opportunities to work outside of traditional office spaces or the typical 9 to 5 desk job. Community colleges offer exciting and varied ways for students to test the waters and explore their personal and career interests, which may be outside of the norm in terms of college majors. For example, plant lovers who want to work outdoors can earn a certificate in landscape design, which will help them gain the knowledge and skills necessary for an entry-level position in a landscape company. California's College of the Sequoias (COS) offers many opportunities for students to study unique certificate pathways that align with their interests and skill sets. Landscape Design, Ornamental Horticulture, Floral Technology, Animal Science, Architectural Visual Communication: these are just a few of the certificates offered by COS (see https://www.cos.edu.en-us/). Such options can meet the niche needs of the marketplace and consumers. In short, the local community college might offer just the unique pathway a student is seeking.

Technology is a major area of economic and career growth. According to the U.S. Bureau of Labor Statistics (2023), computer and information technology (IT) careers are expected to grow significantly between 2022 and 2032, outpacing the growth of other occupations. In addition to the industry growth, new workers will be needed to fill new and/or vacated positions. Community colleges anticipate this need and offer many options to students to gain the required skills to step into these roles. Local colleges are adept at forming partnerships with local industry leaders to provide the appropriate training and employees for local economies.

Certifications

It can be challenging to understand the difference between certificates and certifications. In fact, often these terms are conflated. Being clear about the differences between certificates and certifications is important for prospective students, and in this section, we aim to cultivate that understanding. Certificates represent completing a set of learning objectives from educational or training programs. Certifications are awarded by third-party assessors based on a proven competency that is separate from the educational experience. Certifications are generally time-bound, based on skill sets defined by industry standards, and require recertification to maintain the certified status. Certifications can be revoked in cases of unethical or demonstrations of incompetent behavior. The opportunity to take a certification exam may depend upon completing education and/or a training program where students can learn the skills at the community college and go on to complete the industry certification—often sitting for a test to show competency. Some certifications may also include a specified number of weeks, months, or years of experience prior to sitting for the exam.

Today's IT certification options seem endless. It is likely these options will continue to grow. Entry-level IT Fundamentals and Solutions Architect certifications are often part of an IT certification roadmap. Bundles of certifications are often necessary to keep pace with an ever-changing IT landscape. There are systems certifications, hardware certifications, cloud certifications, plus many more. Often community colleges partner with third-party testing organizations to offer the training and skills necessary to help students pass certification exams. For example, Reynolds Community College in Richmond, Virginia, helps students prepare to sit for certification exams in multiple areas, such as CIW Web Design Specialist, A+, Network+, and more. See https://www.reynolds.edu/get_started/programs/ist/certifications.html.

Maricopa Community College in Arizona offers over 50 IT certificates and certifications, some of which can be completed in just two semesters. Some options include Computer System Configuration and Support, Blockchain Technology, and Amazon Web Services Cloud Specialist. These credentials enable students to specialize in IT and enter the job market with little student debt. See https://www.maricopa.edu/degrees-certificates/computer-information-technology. In a partnership between Wake Technical Community College in North Carolina, Google Cloud and Deutsche Bank helped students gain skills and talents and have direct pipeline access to connect with local high-paying job opportunities, especially in the Research Triangle area of North Carolina, which includes Raleigh, Durham, and Chapel Hill (Elenez, 2022).

Licenses

Students often imagine and aspire toward high-paying careers that do not require a four-year degree. Some of these career choices do, however, require government licensing. Licenses often accompany formal education programs and are awarded by a governmental agency after demonstration of an expected skill or competency. Licenses generally cover a specific skill in a defined area. They can be revoked, and often must be renewed. Licensed career paths include licensed practical nurses (LPNs), licensed electricians, licensed cosmetologists, licensed teachers, and licensed building contractors. Community colleges can offer courses to prepare candidates for their licensing exams. Often, students may pursue a certificate or associate degree program with the chance to take the licensing exam at the end of the coursework. This is a great opportunity for students to enter an industry, become licensed, and pursue a career goal without spending extensive time or money.

Degrees

Of course, students interested in specific career-focused programs may also want to pursue a college degree, an associate or bachelor's degree. Not all associate's degrees are the same. Similarly, not all bachelor's degrees are the same. Degrees such as the Associate of Applied Science (AAS) indicate a curricular focus on workforce competency and immediate entry into a career. On the other hand, an Associate of Arts (AA) degree indicates a focus on general education courses meant to provide students with a more holistic educational experience through the liberal arts and preparation for transfer. These nuances should be examined and understood by prospective students (see Chapter 5 for additional information and helpful definitions). While most community colleges operate on an open-access imperative, meaning all prospective students may enroll, not all community college *programs* are open-access. In fact, some programs are highly competitive—sometimes more so than similar programs at four-year institutions. Prospective students should ask their academic advisors about program-level acceptance rates when considering the community college option.

As mentioned above, some community colleges offer bachelor's degrees in high-demand career areas. Many of these degrees are applied. For example, the College of Southern Nevada offers a Bachelor of Applied Science (BAS) degree in Cardiorespiratory Sciences (see https://catalog.csn.edu/preview_program.php?catoid=11&poid=5063). Depending on their location, students may have access to such community college baccalaureate programs. Pursuing a bachelor's degree through a community college can be much more affordable than doing so through a four-year college or university. However, many of these workforce-focused programs are extremely competitive. Prospective students should have a clear understanding of the accessibility of such opportunities.

Apprenticeships
Another approach to career education is through an apprenticeship. Apprenticeship opportunities vary widely from community to community, yet many community colleges help facilitate apprenticeship programs. The U.S. Department of Labor offers helpful resources on this topic (see https://www.apprenticeship.gov/). Furthermore, the American Association of Community Colleges (AACC) has become more actively involved in supporting and expanding community college apprenticeship programs. Such programs are available in many fields, such as healthcare, early childhood education, and advanced manufacturing. Most apprenticeships are concentrated in the skilled trades. Some examples include plumbing, tool and die making, machine repair, and robotics. These valuable learning opportunities are expanding into knowledge work as well. The Maine Apprenticeship Program offers one example: https://www.maine.gov/labor/jobs_training/apprenticeship/. These opportunities provide students with a chance to *learn and earn*—often with benefits, making the experience not only affordable, but profitable. Registered apprenticeship

programs (RAPs) are nationally recognized and portable credentials. Learn more at: https://www.apprenticeship.gov/employers/registered-apprenticeship-program.

Career Readiness

As stated in the opening of this chapter, preparing for the workforce is not easy for anyone, let alone a newly graduated high school student. Thankfully, community colleges offer opportunities for students to prepare for work in terms of competencies and skill building. For example, the Lumina Foundation is an independent, private foundation that partners with colleges and universities to help high school students have easier and more direct access to higher education. Details can be found at: https://www.luminafoundation.org/. This organization strongly emphasizes supporting students from low socioeconomic and marginalized backgrounds who have not had access to the training and skills they need for jobs with livable wages. The Lumina Foundation uses evidence-based information to address state and federal policymakers in creating a more equitable system for training employees to work in a global economy. In addition, the Lumina Foundation has studied significant aspects of education and training that align with society's economic needs to ensure students are successful when entering the workforce.

It might help to consider the community college as a testing ground and a place to overcome any perceptions or misconceptions prospective students and others may have regarding professionalism in the workplace. How should one act and dress on the job, and how does one convey readiness for the position during the first job interview? This varies from one job to another. Many students may lack this perspective. Community colleges are great places for students to develop the myriad skills they will need to thrive in the job market and workplace. For example, the local community colleges can help students prepare for their first job interview and create a stand-out resume and LinkedIn profile. With the growing shift to online learning and support, career development offices are now offering webinars, web-based toolkits, and Zoom sessions to engage with their students and campus community. Remote assistance can be helpful to busy students or those unable to travel to campus. Davidson-Davie Community College in Thomasville, North Carolina, has an Office of Career Development that provides opportunities for advising sessions, interviews, professional attire preparation, and job search exploration (see https://www.davidsondavie.edu/student-life/student-resources/career-development/). Additionally, students can submit resumes to the Office of Career Development website and receive written feedback. Like many other institutions, Davidson-Davie Community College has developed a robust online career readiness presence with links to several different websites to help prepare students for the workforce. For example, one resource they share is CareerOneStop (https://www.careeronestop.org/), which provides information on career options, salaries, and training or certifications. The Office has several professional staff members dedicated to assisting with career readiness between counseling sessions and high school career coaching; the team strives to prepare their students by engaging with the local community before they even attend college. It is helpful to reverse engineer your degree based on your strengths, interests, and career aspirations (see Chapter 5 for more information and tips). Further, it is important for all students to visit with career center personnel to ensure they are making the best possible academic decisions.

Preparing one's resume and applying for a job are some of the first steps to employment; however, many students do not have experience preparing for an interview. Some students cannot afford professional clothing items they rarely use—such as blazers and dress slacks or skirts which are traditionally worn at job interviews. Thankfully, many community college career centers offer some version of a *Dress for Success* program where community members donate new or like-new professional or business casual attire for students to access. Career Centers at Southwestern Community College in Sylvia, North Carolina, host a Dress for Success program through their Career Closet, where students can access clothing items, shoes, and accessories. See https://www.southwesterncc.edu/career-services. Career preparedness—no matter when students enter the workforce—is an essential resource for community college students. Knowing this, community colleges invest time, resources, and professional staff to help implement these career-supporting initiatives for students.

Summary

In this chapter, we explored the role of community colleges in providing workforce education and development opportunities through higher education. Community colleges offer a variety of programs, including accelerated and condensed semesters, specific trade certifications, specialized certificates, and two-year associate degrees. These institutions focus not only on academic degrees but also on vocational training and skill development to meet the demands of the local job market. We highlighted the importance of community college and industry partnerships in preparing students for work through collaboration, internships, apprenticeships, and job opportunities. Additionally, we emphasized the benefits of condensed semesters, such as accelerated programs and micro-credentials, which provide students with a quicker route to completion and more specialized learning options that can lead to swifter entry into the workforce. By aligning curriculum with industry needs, community colleges ensure that their graduates are well prepared and have the relevant skills for employment. Additionally, because community college credentials can often be stacked, students can take their education one step at a time and earn the credentials they need when they are required.

Discussion and Reflection Prompts

Support Prompts

◆ List what you know about advising students on workforce education and development. Where are the gaps, and how can you learn more?

◆ What kinds of sub-associate educational opportunities are available at your local community college?

- What is your local economy like? In what businesses or industries do most people work? Check out the Bureau of Labor Statistics to learn more (https://www.bls.gov/). How can that knowledge empower your students?
- What do you know about apprenticeship opportunities in your area? What is the best way to share this pathway with students?

Student Prompts

- What career paths interest you, and why?
- What information do you need to feel successful in identifying the best educational journey in support of your ideal first job or career?
- Who in your family or school might you speak with about your career interests?

References

Brownlee, M. I. (2023, March 23). The power of microcredentials and America's higher education dilemma. *EdSurge.* https://www.edsurge.com/news/2023-03-23-the-power-of-microcredentials-and-america-s-higher-education-dilemma

Burke, L. (2022, April 28). Many certificate programs don't pay off, but colleges want to keep offering them anyway. *The Hechinger Report.* Available at: https://hechingerreport.org/many-certificate-programs-dont-pay-off-but-colleges-want-to-keep-offering-them-anyway/

City College of New York. (n.d.). ASAP at a glance. Available at: https://www1.cuny.edu/sites/asap/about/asap-at-a-glance/

Elenez, B. (2022, December 22). Deutsche Bank, Wake Technical Community College, and Google Cloud are building a cloud talent pipeline in North Carolina. Google Cloud Blog. Available at: https://cloud.google.com/blog/topics/public-sector/deutsche-bank-wake-technical-community-college-and-google-cloud-are-building-cloud-talent-pipeline-north-carolina/

Myers, J. E., & Kellogg, K. C. (2022). State actor orchestration for achieving workforce development at scale: Evidence from four US states. *ILR Review, 75*(1), 28–55. https://doi.org/10.1177/0019793920942767

Ruf, J. (2021, June 2). Rethinking the 16-week semester: Is a shorter semester more equitable? And for whom? *Diverse*. https://www .diverseeducation.com/institutions/community-colleges/article /15109361/rethinking-the-16-week-semester-is-a-shorter-semester -more-equitable-and-for-whom

U.S. Bureau of Labor Statistics. (2023, September 6). Employment projections: 2022–2032 summary. *Economic News Release*. Available at: https://www.bls.gov/news.release/ecopro.nr0.htm

5

The Community College Academic Experience

Choosing a college can be a daunting experience for students and their families. Often, students are inundated with information from their peers, family members, social media, and high school counselors. While the community college may not be the first institution high achieving students consider, it may be the best option for those who wish to stay closer to home and save money. As students consider enrolling in their local community college, it is important they focus on the academic experience and transfer options available to them once they finish their program. Academic options should align closely with a student's short- and longer-term goals—either transfer to a four-year institution or more immediate employability. The key is understanding *what* to study, *how* that study aligns with career plans, *which* academic programs are available at the local community college, and *where* students hope to transfer afterwards.

The good news is students do not have to have everything figured out from Day 1. In fact, many community college credentials (degrees and certificates) are stackable and portable, which means students can build their degrees, starting with a short-term certificate and finishing with a transferable two-year degree. While a community college advisor will help guide students toward completing their degree, remember, a two-year degree may simply be a springboard—so in a sense, the pressure

DOI: 10.4324/9781003346210-5

is off. If, however, a student is confident in their longer-term transfer and academic goals, they may consider planning strategies that include a reverse-engineered approach where students start with the *end* in mind—the baccalaureate degree—and work backwards. This approach can help students determine ideal majors and course choices at the community college level and minimize the chance of taking courses that do not apply to their major at the four-year institution. Again, not all students will have a crystal-clear idea of their longer-term goals, and that is alright. In this case, students cannot go wrong by taking the first step toward a college degree at their local community college.

A key step in selecting a community college should include assessing the academic experience and transfer opportunities. Here, a one-size-fits-all approach does not work. In this chapter, we help high achieving students assess the quality of a two-year curriculum by examining academic rigor and portability for transfer. Understanding the types of credentials offered at the local community college and how they transfer to four-year colleges and universities is important. Learning within intimate community college classrooms, where faculty to student ratios are low, is powerful. The average community college class size is around 30 students (Kisker et al., 2023), whereas university lecture halls, often led by a teaching assistant and not a full-time faculty member, may hold hundreds of students. And while many community college faculty members are part-time instructors rather than full-time faculty, their expertise in the field and low student-to-faculty ratio provide an excellent opportunity for students to engage and learn from their faculty in ways that may not be possible in large four-year institution settings.

There is evidence to show that students who transfer to a four-year institution after earning a two-year degree perform better than students who start at the four-year institution (Xu et al., 2018). In this chapter, we highlight some of the factors that play into this positive student outcome, for example, talented community college faculty, who, though they may be part-time instructors, bring real-world experiences into their classrooms, which is invaluable to students. In addition, some of the best-kept secrets at community colleges are High Impact Programs

(HIPs), such as honors programs, where students can feel like they attend a college within a college, which adds community and connectedness. In these programs, students receive additional support and participate in learning experiences, such as internships, writing-intensive courses, and undergraduate research, which are known to increase retention and student success (American Association of Colleges & Universities, 2023). HIPs and small learning communities, such as honors programs, may be a great fit for high achieving students. Learners can enroll in one of the country's community college honors programs, where students receive an enhanced academic experience. Ivy Tech Community College in Indiana, Miami Dade College in Florida, and Cuyahoga Community College in Ohio are examples of robust two-year honors programs. Also in this chapter, we provide information to help readers understand accreditation in higher education—and explain why this matters and how it impacts students. Examples of students impacted in the transfer process when courses are taken at an unaccredited institution are included. We also discuss reverse transfer opportunities that may be available, which is a unique opportunity where students who transfer before completing an associate degree can complete a two-year credential even after they transfer to a four-year institution.

Terminology

Let us first start with reviewing and providing some important terms and definitions used in higher education. Prospective students and their families can better navigate college and transfer in general by familiarizing themselves with commonly used terminology and definitions such as below:

◆ *Associate Degree*: A degree granted by an institution of higher education after the completion of a two-year program (approximately 60 credits) of study, including but not limited to the Associate of Arts (A.A.), the Associate of Science (A.S.), and the Associate of Applied Science (A.A.S.).

◆ *Associate of General Studies (AGS)*: The Associate of General Studies is an associate degree offered by many community colleges. As the name suggests, it is a general program that does not have as many specific requirements as the Associate of Arts or the Associate of Science. This degree program allows students to customize their curriculum and take classes that best meet their unique career goals. General Studies often works well when students reverse engineer their four-year degree where they can leverage the flexibility of the AGS degree to meet both long- and short-term degree requirements.

◆ *Associate of Fine Arts (AFA)*: A two-year program that is generally designed for transfer to a bachelor's program or for students who seek to begin entry-level or freelance work. Some institutions require a portfolio of the applicant's work.

◆ *Bachelor's Degree*: A degree granted by an institution of higher education after the completion of a four-year program (approximately 120 credits) of study, including the Bachelor of Arts (B.A.) and the Bachelor of Science (B.S.).

◆ *Certificate*: Certificates are popular often because they can be obtained quickly. Most certificate programs take only one year to complete, or as little as a few weeks in some cases. Certificates may be connected to specific industry standards, such as a Microsoft certification in computer science, or prepare students for state certifications, such as massage therapist or cosmetology certifications. Certification requirements may differ from state to state and institution to institution. Also, a certificate and a certification are not always the same thing.

◆ *Technical Certificate (TC)*: Community college certificate programs are relatively short-term, lasting anywhere from a few months to a year. They cost less than four-year degrees and have higher completion rates relative to degree programs. TCs offer specialized education and training that allow students to develop transferable skill sets specific to the work field or type of job they aim to follow. TCs enable students to study their desired area of focus and graduate in a shorter time frame with job-ready skills.

◆ *Micro-credential*: Micro-credentials recognize short-duration, competency-based learning opportunities that align with labor market or community needs and can be assessed and recognized for employment or further learning opportunities. This type of credential is growing in popularity.

◆ *Articulation*: According to Kamen (2022), articulation is "the process of equating coursework between institutions" (para. 3). This may happen at the course or program level. Articulation may also be necessary for international postsecondary coursework or credit by exam. For a state-by-state comparison of transfer and articulation policies, students might start their research at: https://www.ecs .org/50-state-comparison-transfer-and-articulation/.

◆ *Swirlers*: This designation is used for undergraduate students who move between two- and four-year institutions. Swirlers may attend a four-year institution, then enroll in a community college, then move back into a four-year institution.

◆ *Visiting/Guest Student Status*: Community colleges are often the *go-to* institution for four-year students who wish to pick up a lower-cost or more flexible course at some point in their education, often during a summer term. Community colleges have long offered courses to meet the needs of diverse learners—online, virtual, accelerated, and so on. Students must ensure the course they wish to take at a community college is transferable not only to their four-year institution generally but also to their program of study specifically.

◆ *Guaranteed Admissions Agreements*: Once students complete an associate degree, they are automatically accepted at the four-year institution if a Guaranteed Admissions Agreement is in place. It is important to note, however, that sometimes these types of agreements are limited to specific degrees. New Hampshire, Hawaii, Kansas, Indiana, Kentucky, Oregon, Florida, and California are among several states with these agreements. Because there may be certain requirements such as grade expectations in classes as well as a minimum GPA at the time of graduation, students are encouraged to fully understand the Guaranteed Admissions Agreements at their institutions.

For additional transfer resources, we encourage students to visit College Transfer.Net at https://www.collegetransfer.net/ Transfer-Home/Glossary-of-College-Transfer-Terms. Remember, the takeaway here is it is never too early for any community college-bound student to begin thinking about transfer.

Accreditation

In the early stages of college exploration, it is important to consider an institution's accreditation status, as this will impact the transferability of the courses, and in some cases, the programs and careers students wish to pursue. It can be devastating when students learn they cannot transfer credits—classes they have taken, degrees they have earned, money they have spent—because the receiving institution does not share the same or reciprocal accreditation. Colleges and universities in the U.S. are evaluated by both regional and national agencies to ensure they meet minimum quality and academic standards. The most recognized and accepted accreditation is regional. Typically, colleges will only guarantee that they will accept transfer credits from *regionally accredited* institutions. The six regional accreditation bodies in the U.S. are:

- ◆ Accrediting Commission for Community and Junior Colleges (ACCJC) Western Association of Schools and Colleges (WASC);
- ◆ Higher Learning Commission (HLC);
- ◆ New England Commission of Higher Education (NECHE);
- ◆ Northwest Commission on Colleges and Universities (NWCCU);

- ◆ Southern Association of Colleges and Schools Commission on Colleges (SACSA);
- ◆ WASC Senior College and University Commission (WSCUC).

More information on accrediting bodies can be found at: https://www.chea.org/regional-accrediting-organizations. These agencies are recognized by the Council on Higher Education Accreditation and/or the U.S. Department of Education. Accreditation aims to ensure students are provided with a high-quality education that meets specific standards. While these acronyms may sound like a foreign language to students and their families, they matter and should be considered. Students should seek to attend schools that will provide them with a high-quality education along with credits that transfer. Knowing your school is in good standing with one of these accrediting bodies provides a level of assurance that you will receive a quality college education.

All institutions of higher education should prominently include information regarding their accreditation status on their website. And again, it is important to look for this information. If you cannot locate this information, the institution may not be accredited or may have lost its accreditation because of issues they failed to rectify. In other cases, an institution may not have the accreditation you need to transfer to your preferred four-year college or university. For example, Walla Walla Community College is NWCCU accredited, and the information is readily available at: https://www.wwcc.edu/about/accreditation/. NWCCU accreditation means their classes and degree programs are likely transferable to other regionally accredited institutions such as Washington State University or Seattle University.

It is also important to understand that some programs and degree types may also have programmatic accreditation in addition to regional accreditation, which happens at the institutional level. For example, the two most prominent nursing accreditation agencies are the Accreditation Commission for Education in Nursing or ACEN (https://www.acenursing.org) and the Commission on Collegiate Nursing Education or CCNE (https://

www.aacnnursing.org/ccne-accreditation). In some cases, a student may not be hired by an employer without completing a program with the appropriate accreditation. Think of these accreditations as stamps of approval that validate the quality of the nursing curriculum and education. For more information regarding nursing accreditation, visit https://nursinglicensemap .com/nursing-degrees/nursing-accreditation/.

In addition to the transfer of credit, a student's financial aid may be impacted by a school's accreditation status. Further, the line of work a student wishes to pursue, such as nursing, as explained above, may require the institution and program to be accredited by a particular accrediting body. Some online institutions or trade schools may not be accredited in the same way; therefore, it is always good practice for prospective students to do their homework and check for reciprocity if they wish to transfer to a regionally accredited four-year institution after attending a community college. Students studying at an unaccredited institution may not be eligible for financial aid, including student loans, through a governmental agency, so it is important to review an institution's ability to issue financial aid. For additional information regarding institutional eligibility, visit the most recent issue of the *Federal Student Aid Handbook,* see https://fsapartners.ed.gov /knowledge-center/fsa-handbook/2023-2024. More on this topic is included in Chapter 6.

Institutions that cannot demonstrate recognized accreditation may be referred to as *diploma mills.* Ultimately, it will be a student's receiving institution—the college or university they wish to transfer to after community college—that will decide whether they will or will not accept the transfer credits. The bottom line is it is important to know how credits earned at the local community college will transfer to a student's chosen receiving institution. We cannot overstate the importance of due diligence when it comes to ensuring your selected institution and program offer significant, legitimate academic work. Relatedly, employers too may look more favorably at an applicant who attended an accredited institution. To learn more about accreditation, visit the Council for Higher Education Accreditation at: https://www.chea.org/directory-chea -recognized-accrediting-organizations-pdf.

Interests and Learning Preferences

Once students validate accreditation status and reciprocity among their selected institutions(s), they will want to understand what their community college offers in terms of classes and degree programs. For students who are unsure of what they wish to study or major in, many resources are available at the community college to help them select an area of interest. This does not mean students cannot take a detour or two along their academic and career journey; rather, it means this is where students will start. The less often students change majors, the quicker they can finish their credential and transfer or enter the workforce. Community college career and advising centers help guide students in directing their interests and talents and to understand how their strengths and goals align with the available programs at the school. This process may include interest and skills inventories and other assessment instruments. Such tools not only help students explore careers but also help them better understand themselves as learners including how they learn best, commonly referred to as learning preferences. This sometimes overlooked step in the admissions process can mean the difference between striving and thriving in college. A bit of work before declaring a major can help prospective students better align their interests and aspirations with an appropriate major during their first two years of college. Career research tools and career assessments such as those found on the Portland Community College website (see https://www.pcc.edu/careers/career-exploration/) are important early steps in preparing for college. Valencia College in Florida provides another example of a robust Career Center that helps students explore their interests and employment aspirations (see https://valenciacollege.edu/students/career-center/self-exploration.php).

Articulations

Once students have an idea of their career interests and learning preferences, they will need to align those interests with a major or pathway at their local community college. The best way for prospective students to learn about academic options at a particular community college is to visit their website, where they will look for the *Academics* or *Programs* tab. Here is where they will see the degree programs offered and the curriculum to finish a degree and/or certificate. And while the variety of degree choices may confuse students, here are a few tips. As noted earlier in this chapter, the primary difference between associate degrees is that the Associate of Applied Science (AAS) degree, for example, focuses on vocational skills training and preparation for immediate employment. In contrast, the Associate of Arts (AA), Associate of Science (AS), Associate of Fine Arts (AFA), and Associate of General Studies (AGS) degrees are designed for students who plan to transfer to a four-year program. The two-year AA, AS, AFA, and AGS degrees are particularly useful for high achieving students who believe community college can offer a cost-savings springboard on their way to earning a four-year degree. It is important to note that applied (AAS) degrees also may transfer to four-year institutions, however, the curriculum often focuses on technical competencies rather than general education core competencies. As such, the amount of transferable credit may fall short of 60 credit hours. Simply put, an AAS degree may not shave-off two years of a four-year degree in the same way that AA, AFA, AS, and AGS degrees are designed to do. Transfer articulation agreements between two- and four-year institutions are co-created between institutions to facilitate 2+2 opportunities (two years at the community college + two years at a university = a bachelor's degree). So, if a student's goal is to enroll in a program that transfers seamlessly to a four-year institution, the 2+2 pathway should be fully examined. Most institutions post articulation and transfer information on their websites. Advisors and admission representatives are also able to provide information.

Some high achieving students will seek to gain technical and vocational skills at a two-year college and therefore may choose to focus on a pathway that leads to a career such as a web developer, dental hygienist, radiation therapist, traffic controller, or computer help desk technician. At any community college, there will be many choices to explore in the technical and vocational areas. Certificates and applied degrees allow graduates to enter the workforce sooner and with less college expense. Many students will begin their career with a two-year credential and return to school later to complete additional degrees. In short, students can stack credentials and earn additional degrees and certificates when they choose to do so. This approach can help a student take college one step at a time. Academic and transfer advisors can help students select stackable and transferable credentials. One high-profile example of such a matriculation pattern is Ileana Ros-Lehtinen. Ros-Lehtinen is a Cuban immigrant who became the first Hispanic woman voted into Congress in 1989, where she served until 2019. Ros-Lehtinen earned an associate degree from Miami Dade College and then transferred to Florida International University where she completed a bachelor's degree. While this is just one example, it reminds us to consider the vast array of students who begin their academic journeys at the community college.

As stated previously, many schools have established 2+2 transfer agreements that facilitate transfer for students. These agreements aim to make transfer seamless between two- and four-year institutions where students take only the classes they need to complete a two-year degree and transfer as a junior at their receiving institution. Typically, this means a student will earn 60 credit hours at the community college and 60 more at the baccalaureate institution. Most four-year degrees require 120 earned credit hours to graduate. Any credits above the requirement equate to more time and money in college. These agreements help prevent students from taking extra courses that do not apply to their majors, thus saving students time and money. While most of these agreements are between community colleges and *public* four-year institutions, students should not overlook transfer agreements between community colleges and private four-year institutions such as Notre Dame University, Creighton University, College of the Atlantic, Duke University, Dartmouth College, and Stanford University.

The bottom line is students should work closely with college academic advisors and transfer experts to ensure they are enrolling in the correct courses and meeting any requirements that could be part of an articulation agreement, such as a minimum GPA at the time of graduation. It is also important to consider that some articulations apply broadly and align with multiple institutions, while others may only apply to certain schools and/or programs. And again, students do not need to count transfer out if they are earning an applied degree (AAS) at their local community college. While an AAS graduate may take more than two years to complete a bachelor's degree after transfer, with good advisement and planning, a pathway can still be forged and mapped out.

Reverse Credit Transfer

Reverse Credit Transfer (RCT) programs have been developed by some institutions to help students complete a credential after they leave their community college without a degree in hand. RCT is an emerging policy designed to award associate degrees to students who transfer from two-year to four-year institutions after transfer (Giani et al., 2021). This means if a student transfers to their four-year college or university before completing a degree or certificate at the two-year institution, they can transfer credits back to their community college once they take the equivalent courses at the four-year institution. In many cases, schools with RCT programs award two-year degrees and credentials automatically and without any action needed by the student. In other cases, students may need to send a copy of their four-year transcript back to their community college upon their completion of the courses needed to complete the two-year credential. Either way, it is through reverse transfer that students can combine the credits they earn at their four-year school with those they had previously earned at community college and retroactively be awarded an associate degree.

This *recover-your-degree* strategy is part of the larger college completion agenda championed by state education departments, private foundations, and national higher education organizations (Nietzel, 2019). Completing an associate degree has been shown to increase a student's overall earning power. The programs students enroll in and whether they complete them are consequential in terms of their future earnings (Jenkins & Weiss, 2011). So, whether a student completes an associate degree in a linear fashion or through reverse transfer, it just makes sense to pursue credential completion. To find out if an institution participates in RCT, ask an admissions or transfer officer.

Guided Pathways

Many community colleges try to help students stay on track to reach their goals by following the Guided Pathways model. Guided Pathways is a nationally recognized initiative that helps ensure equity and improved student outcomes for their students. See here for additional details and information: https://ccrc.tc.columbia .edu/research/guided-pathways.html. In this model, community colleges standardize pathways to help ensure students transfer more seamlessly and take only the courses they need. Often, Guided Pathways schools create meta-majors where academic and career communities bring faculty together to examine their entire curriculum to create a highly transformative learning experience for new degree-seeking students. With the Guided Pathways model, gone are the days of community colleges offering such a wide variety of courses that students get lost in choices and, in turn, take courses that do not transfer. The Guided Pathways program, whether schools formally call it as such, helps students succeed and save time and money toward earning a college degree. Comprehensive institutional reforms such as those deemed necessary in the Guided Pathways model are challenging. Such change requires committed leaders who can engage faculty and staff from across the college. While students may not be aware of such impactful programs being implemented at their community college, what they should understand is that community colleges are always seeking ways to innovate and improve student outcomes.

Community College Baccalaureate Programs

While community colleges offer certificates and two-year degrees, some community colleges offer limited bachelor's degree programs as well. Earning a bachelor's degree at their local community college can be especially helpful to students living in areas with less access to higher education. More can be learned at: https://www.accbd.org/. In one example, Valencia College in Florida offers bachelor's degrees in a select number of areas. Students at the college can extend their education after their associate degree and bachelor's degree in a variety of areas. See https://valenciacollege.edu/future-students/bachelors.php. At Valencia, students are required to complete an associate degree at the college before they are eligible to apply for the four-year program. Four-year degree programs offered at select community colleges will cost more than completing just the associate degree but will still cost much less than tuition and fees at a neighboring university. Columbia Basin College (CBC) in Washington also offers several bachelor's degrees; see https://www.columbiabasin.edu/learn/discover-your-path/bachelor-programs/index.html. Like other community colleges that offer bachelor's degrees, students at CBC must earn their associate degree or have a similar credential or collection of credits to be eligible to apply for a bachelor's degree program.

Community College Faculty

Faculty are at the core of any institution of higher education. This holds true at the community college as well, where faculty focus on teaching and are not often required to engage in research or scholarly endeavors as part of their jobs, though some do. Whether instructors are full- or part-time (adjunct), community college faculty can develop strong relationships with their students because of lower faculty-to-student ratios. Community college classrooms are generally smaller than those at large public universities where introductory courses may be taught in large lecture halls by graduate students. In addition, some faculty choose to work at two-year institutions because they attended one themselves and they feel attached to the community college mission (Borst & Latz, 2020).

Full-time community college faculty play an essential role at their institution and may or may not have tenure. Some faculty are unionized, which can offer additional protections, such as collective bargaining. Faculty salaries at institutions with unions are often higher than for those teaching at a non-union institution. Unlike adjuncts, full-time community college faculty hold regular office hours, serve on committees, and develop curriculum and programs, though some adjunct faculty may participate in this work as well.

The majority of faculty at the community college are part-time instructors. In fact, over half of all community college courses are taught by part-time faculty (adjunct), and the reliance on part-time faculty to teach developmental or remedial courses and gateway math and English courses is even more commonplace (Ran & Sanders, 2020). While utilizing adjunct faculty can help community colleges keep their instruction costs lower, there are both challenges and benefits with this model of staffing courses. One of the greatest challenges in hiring adjunct faculty is their mobility—or lack thereof—and limited ability to teach sections during the day, as many are fully employed outside of the community college. In addition, the availability of part-time faculty can vary from semester to semester, which can be a challenge for course scheduling and long-term program planning. On the flip side, many believe the use of adjunct faculty results in better learning and career networking outcomes for students as they often have instructors working in the *field* who can bring real-world expertise into the classroom learning.

Adjunct faculty are diverse. According to Gappa and Leslie (1993), adjuncts can be categorized as follows: (a) career enders—retired or pre-retired educators who are in transition from established careers; (b) specialist, expert, or professional—those who come from a wide range of fields and careers who typically have a full-time career outside academia; (c) aspiring academics—those who hope for full-time involvement as an academic, and for Gappa and Leslie, this category included part-time faculty with terminal degrees who desire full-time academic careers and all-but-dissertation doctoral students; and (d) freelancers—those whose preference is to work at several different part-time occupations, of which teaching is only one.

Regardless of their employment status (full- or part-time), community college faculty who teach at accredited institutions must meet the credentialing requirements set by their accrediting bodies. Typically, faculty must have an earned master's degree in the discipline they wish to teach, such as Psychology or Mathematics, or a master's degree in a different field with at least 18 graduate-level credit hours in the discipline of the course they will be teaching. Many community college faculty have doctoral degrees, though terminal degrees are not normally required to teach at the community college. Rest assured, community college faculty, whether they teach full- or part-time, meet credentialing requirements—failure to meet these requirements may jeopardize their institution's accreditation status.

High Impact Programs/Practices

As stated at the beginning of this chapter, High Impact Programs/ Practices (HIPs) are educational practices that research has shown can increase rates of retention, engagement, and persistence to graduation for all students across diverse backgrounds. Many families and counselors may not be aware of the variety of high impact programs available at their local community college. High impact programs and practices not only enhance the student experience at the community college but can also better prepare students for success at their baccalaureate/transfer institutions and in their careers. With extra student supports and programming, HIPs can help students feel at home (and better supported) within the larger campus community. For many students, this sense of belonging can be the primary reason they persist in college. Regardless of a student's major, HIPs can provide extensive resources and support to improve a student's two-year experience and outcomes. TRIO, ASAP, and Honors Programs are just a few HIPs aimed at improving the student experience, retention, completion, and transfer outcomes. Likely, your local community college offers a variety of such programs to help you succeed, so be sure to explore all the options with your admissions representative.

TRIO

TRIO is a federally funded grant program that provides direct support services for students, and relevant training for directors and staff. According to their website, TRIO programs have helped America's low-income and first-generation college students access and complete higher education since 1965. TRIO programs provide services to students throughout the education pipeline, as early as middle school, as well as undergraduates interested in pursuing a doctorate degree. More information can be found at: https://ope.ed.gov/programs/mapED/storymaps/trio/. TRIO includes eight programs targeted to serve and assist low-income individuals, first-generation college students, and individuals with disabilities to progress through the academic pipeline from middle school to post-baccalaureate programs. TRIO also includes a training program for directors and staff of TRIO programs. The recipients of the federal grants, *depending on the specific program,* are institutions of higher education, and public and private agencies and organizations, including community-based organizations with experience in serving disadvantaged youth and secondary schools. Students must be eligible to receive services and be accepted into a funded project that serves the institution or school that the student is attending or the area in which they live, in order to be served by one of these programs. For more information, visit: https://www2.ed.gov/about/offices/list/ope/trio/index.html.

ASAP

Some community colleges in states such as Ohio, New York, and Indiana offer an accelerated program designed to fast-track a student's two-year degree. Ivy Tech Community College, a statewide system in Indiana, and the City University of New York (CUNY) both offer the Accelerated Study in Associate Programs (ASAP). In Ohio, Cincinnati State Technical and Community College, Cuyahoga Community College, and Lorain County Community College began offering the ASAP program to their students in 2014 (Sommo et al., 2018). This program leverages mostly eight-week courses rather than the traditional 16-week format and provides comprehensive support for associate-degree community college students who can benefit from a condensed and accelerated degree. While in the program, students receive services including academic tutoring, personal counseling, mentoring, financial guidance, transfer assistance, and other support necessary for educational access and retention. These accelerated models have improved retention and graduation rates among enrolled students (Sommo et al., 2018). While not every community college offers ASAP, they likely offer other High Impact Programs (HIPs) that can enhance a student's experience. As such, students are always encouraged to ask their admissions representative for additional information.

Honors Programs

Community college honors programs may be the perfect choice for high achieving students who wish to start college closer to home and save money, all while being academically challenged and well prepared to transfer to a four-year institution after community college. This approach may seem counterintuitive to the high achieving student who in the past may have only considered beginning their higher education on a four-year residential campus. In a compelling study, Glynn (2019) found that students who transferred from community college to selective colleges, like the Ivy Leagues, graduated at higher rates than those transferring from other four-year institutions—and at equal or higher rates than non-transfer students. It is not just a few extraordinary community colleges sending students to selective universities—84% of community colleges sent at least one exceptional student to a four-year institution in Fall 2016 (Glynn, 2019).

Today's students have different expectations for college, and most of all they want a good job after graduation without amassing huge college debt (Selingo, 2020). Paying less for two years of college that prepare them for a great career may be just what today's high achieving student seeks. Further, getting accepted into a top-ranked institution after community college may be easier, as in this example, with a two-year transcript that is strengthened with honors courses, thus demonstrating increased academic rigor and baccalaureate preparedness. In many cases, an honors program may be the solution for motivated and high achieving students.

Collegiate honors programs are designed to serve the needs of gifted, high-ability, or high achieving undergraduates. Like K-12 gifted programs, collegiate honors programs vary, and no single format or model exists (Byrne, 1998; Nachman, 2017; National Collegiate Honors Council, 2018). There is a shared belief across institutions, however, that the usual classroom experience must be enhanced to help high-ability students realize their potential (Hébert & McBee, 2007). In both two- and four-year institutions, honors education and honors experiences will consist of enriched courses and seminars, smaller-than-average class sizes, increased faculty-student contact, opportunities for student research, leadership development programs, and extracurricular activities.

Admission into honors classes may vary across institutions. Many two- and four-year honors programs allow students and faculty to enter honors contracts where instructors assign and grade honors-level assignments in addition to the required course assignments (Floyd & Holloway, 2006; Nachman, 2017). In other instances, registration for honors courses is limited to honors students, where only admitted honors students can enroll. Some community college honors programs are open to all students, regardless of academic preparation, whereas others are restricted to students who meet certain academic requirements. Admissions criteria, and whether entering freshman only or current students are admissible, depend on the school and its honors program's mission (Nachman, 2017). At most community colleges, current students also may apply to move into an honors program after a successful semester or more of college-level coursework (Floyd & Holloway, 2006).

Participating in a two-year honors college may greatly improve a student's transferability to a top four-year college or university, including those institutions with selective admissions. Students from two-year honors colleges are not only accepted to public and private institutions but also may benefit from H+H (Honors to Honors) articulations, which allows qualified honors students at the community college to transfer directly into the Honors

College at their receiving college or university with junior or year three standing. These articulations often include scholarships, fellowships, and other opportunities that can appeal to high achieving students.

For students with big dreams who wish to transfer to a baccalaureate institution, community college honors programs have much to offer. In fact, many community college honors programs will provide honors students with perks such as: priority registration; specialized honors advising; honors lounges; scholarships; opportunities for undergraduate research; and internships. Yet, perhaps, a student testimonial tells the two-year honors story best:

> *My name is Adrianna, and I graduated from the Honors program at Ivy Tech in 2016. I just wanted to reach out and give encouragement to the current students with finals coming up! I know that college can be incredibly challenging, and I spent a lot of time feeling imposter syndrome during my first year at Ivy Tech and after transferring! However, the sky truly is the limit on your dreams, and I think the Honors program is an amazing resource to help push you forward to achieving your goals!! I transferred to Florida International University after graduating, and I went on to get a degree in Biochemistry. I'm now a first-year medical student, and I constantly use the things I learned during my time at Ivy Tech. Honors taught me that "If your dreams don't scare you, they aren't big enough," and I keep that mantra in my head all the time! I believe in you all! Good luck with your upcoming finals!*
>
> (Adrianna N., 2016 Honors College
> Graduate, Ivy Tech Community
> College, Indiana)

High achieving students should not rule out taking honors courses and/or applying to the honors program if their local community college offers this option. This High Impact Program can help students take their community college experience to the next level, thus helping them reach their fullest potential.

Emerging Community College Models

The community college landscape in the U.S. is an ever-changing one. Two examples of the ongoing evolution of the community college model are The Come to Believe Model (CTB) (see https://www.ctbnetwork.org/) and Campus (see https://campus.edu/). The CTB is a two-year degree program embedded within a four-year institution. This model aims to provide support to high achieving and low-income students toward an associate degree and easy access to move into a bachelor's program at a prestigious four-year institution. Some current host institutions include Butler University, Loyola University, Chicago, and the University of Saint Thomas. *Campus* is based in Sacramento, California, and offers limited associate degree and diploma programs. Campus is led by an entrepreneurial-minded team of academic leaders and investors as well as a Board of Trustees populated with seasoned community college leaders. The future and staying power of both of these newer ventures are yet to be seen.

Summary

In this chapter, we explored the academic experience at the community college and offered readers important information related to accreditation, articulation, and transfer. We discussed stackable, short-term credentials that allow students to take smaller steps into college. In addition, we provided a glimpse into the profile of community college faculty and highlighted their role as teachers first, whereas at four-year institutions, research and scholarship can take precedence over teaching. Class sizes are small, and community college faculty usually know their students well. In addition, two-year faculty often work in areas related to their teaching, which means they bring real-world experience into the classroom. We recommended that students who know where they wish to transfer should plan their postsecondary education backwards with the end in mind. We referred to this as reverse engineering your academic journey. This approach can help students stay on track, enroll only in courses that transfer, and complete their degree without a loss of credit. Finally, we highlighted several High Impact Programs (HIPs), such as TRIO, ASAP, and Honors Programs, which can both support and propel community college students to success.

Discussion and Reflection Prompts

Support Prompts

◆ Locate information about whether your local community college offers an honors program. If it does not, determine the closest community college with an honors program, then discover the costs of attendance for your students, as the college may be outside your local geo-political area. What did you learn?

◆ How might you best share this information with the high achieving students you support?

◆ Does your local community college engage in High Impact Programs (HIPs)? How might you connect students with this information?

Student Prompts

◆ Visit the following website and research three potential colleges or universities you may wish to attend. After visiting the website, discuss your findings with your high school counselor or family member and consider the cost of tuition, school ranking (if ranked), and degrees offered: https://www.usnews.com/usnews/store/college_compass?src=web:col_compass:na:profile_admissions_blurb:20201003

◆ Next, research your local community college and determine if they have transfer agreements with the schools you selected above.

◆ Finally, research your community college to determine what short-term credentials might help you get started in college.

References

American Association of Colleges & Universities. (2023, July 6). *High-impact practices*. Available at: https://www.aacu.org/trending-topics/high-impact

Borst, M. B., & Latz, A. O. (2020). Community college faculty experiences in an honors program: A phenomenological study. *Journal of Applied Research in the Community College, 27*(1), 129–147.

Byrne, J. P. (1998). Honors programs in community colleges: A review of recent issues and literature. *Community College Review, 26*(2), 67–81. https://doi.org/10.1177/009155219802600205

Floyd, D. L., & Holloway, A. (2006). Prioritizing service to the academically talented: The honors college. *New Directions for Community Colleges, 136*, 43–52. https://www.doi.org/10.1002/cc.258

Gappa, J. M., & Leslie, D. W. (1993). *The invisible faculty: Improving the status of part-timers in higher education*. Jossey-Bass.

Giani, M., Taylor, J. L., & Kauppila, S. (2021). Examining the educational and employment outcomes of reverse credit transfer. *AERA Open, 7*. https://doi.org/10.1177/2332858421989998

Glynn, J. (2019, January). Persistence: The success of students who transfer from community colleges to selective four-year institutions. Jack Kent Cooke Foundation. Available at: https://www.jkcf.org/research/persistence/

Hébert, T. P., & McBee, M. T. (2007). The impact of an undergraduate honors program on gifted university students. *Gifted Child Quarterly, 51*(2), 136–151. https://www.doi.org/10.1177/0016986207299471

Jenkins, D., & Weiss, M. J. (2011). Charting pathways to completion for low-income community college students (CCRC Working Paper No. 34). Columbia University, Teachers College, Community College Research Center. Available at: https://ccrc.tc.columbia.edu/publications/charting-pathways-to-completion.html

Kamen, S. M. (2022, May 31). *Defining transfer*. American Association of Collegiate Registrars and Admissions Officers. Available at: https://www.aacrao.org/resources/newsletters-blogs/aacrao-connect/article/defining-transfer

Kisker, C. B., Cohen, A. M., & Brawer, F. B. (2023). *The American community college* (7th ed.). Jossey-Bass.

Nachman, B. (2017). Bridging the academic gap. In R. W. Glover & K. M. O'Flaherty (Eds.), *Structural challenges and the future of honors education (Honors education in transition)* (pp. 37–64). Rowman & Littlefield.

National Collegiate Honors Council. (2018). *About NCHC.* Available at: http://www.nchchonors.org/about-nchc

Nietzel, M. T. (2019, February 19). Reverse transfer: A second chance at a first degree. *Forbes.* https://www.forbes.com/sites/michaeltnietzel /2019/02/19/reverse-transfer-a-second-chance-at-a-first-degree/?sh =3c0b89c37bea

Ran, F. X., & Sanders, J. (2020). Instruction quality or working condition? The effects of part-time faculty on student academic outcomes in community college introductory courses. *AERA Open, 6*(1). https:// doi.org/10.1177/2332858420901495

Selingo, J. (2020). *Who gets in and why: A year inside college admissions.* Scribner.

Sommo, C., Cullinan, D., Manno, M., Blake, S., & Alonzo, E. (2018). Doubling graduation rates in a new state: Two-year findings from the ASAP Ohio demonstration. *New York: MDRC, Policy Brief.* https://files.eric.ed .gov/fulltext/ED592008.pdf

Xu, D., Jaggers, S. S., Fletcher, J., & Fink, J. E. (2018). Are community college transfer students "a good bet" for 4-year admissions? Comparing academic and labor market outcomes between transfer and native 4-year college students. *The Journal of Higher Education, 89*(4), 478–502. https://doi.org/10.1080/00221546.2018.1434280

6

Community College Is Affordable, *Not* Inferior

The community college is typically the most affordable option among higher education institutions. While both community colleges and four-year institutions offer academic programs and degrees, the average cost of attending community college in the U.S. is significantly lower than the cost of attending a four-year college or university. These cost savings, however, do not equate to an inferior education. While community colleges are not ranked in the same way four-year schools may be, they do offer quality degrees that transfer to many baccalaureate-granting institutions. In short, a student's local community college will offer degrees that have currency in terms of transfer and career readiness. If a student's ultimate goal is to earn a degree from a university, they can reduce their overall cost by transferring credits earned at a community college to a baccalaureate-granting institution while also preparing themselves for the rigor of a four-year experience.

Price of Community College

The average tuition and fees for public community college in 2023–2024 ranged from $1,440 in California to $8,660 in Vermont (Ma & Pender, 2023). This contrasts with public four-year

DOI: 10.4324/9781003346210-6

institutions, where the average cost of tuition and fees ranged from $6,360 in Florida to $20,370 in Vermont (Ma & Pender, 2023). It is important to note that these are just averages, and the actual cost of attending community college can vary greatly, depending on the location and institution. Additionally, the cost of attending community college can also be affected by factors such as housing, transportation, books, and supplies, so it is important to consider all these expenses when determining the total cost of attendance.

There are a variety of ways to learn about the actual cost of attending a community college. The Department of Education offers an interactive College Map of the U.S. where students can research the price of attending community colleges and universities, both public and private. Visit this website: https://nces .ed.gov/ipeds/collegemap/ and use the search box to get a list of all the colleges, including community colleges. The results include various data points to help students understand in-state and out-of-state tuition and fees, student population, types of degrees offered, campus settings and housing options, and the college's physical address. To find the most up-to-date and reliable information, students should always visit the college's website.

To be sure, most colleges have information about tuition, fees, and other costs related to attendance on their websites. Typically, this information can be found on a college website by searching for the college's cost calculator or net price calculator. A community college net price calculator is an online tool that provides students and their families with an estimate of the cost of attending a specific community college after accounting for estimated scholarships, grants, and financial aid from federal, state, and local government sources. This tool is designed to help students and families understand their out-of-pocket expenses and make informed decisions about college affordability. The calculator typically asks for information such as family income, assets, number of family members, and the number of children attending college. Based on this information, the calculator provides an estimate of the cost of attendance, including tuition, fees, room and board, books and supplies, and other expenses.

The calculation tool also provides an estimate of the financial aid that may be available, such as scholarships, grants, and student loans. Students and families may also find U.S. colleges' net price calculators by visiting the following website: https://collegecost .ed.gov/net-price.

Another reliable source of information is to contact the college's financial aid office directly. Every community college has a financial aid office which is responsible for administering and managing student financial aid programs. The financial aid office helps students and their families understand the cost of attendance and provides information and guidance regarding the different types of financial aid available, including federal and state aid, scholarships, grants, work-study programs, and student loans. This office is also responsible for reviewing and processing financial aid applications, determining eligibility, and awarding financial aid to students. In addition, they may also offer resources and support to help students understand the process of financial aid, complete the Free Application for Federal Student Aid (FAFSA), and manage their student loan debt. It is always advised that students start the FAFSA process early to maximize their eligibility for aid.

Paying for Community College

Not only is attending community college an affordable option, there are also resources available to help pay for a two-year education. These resources range from federal and state grants and scholarships to local community resources, including financial aid at the community college that may cover not only tuition and fees but also, in some cases, books, living expenses, or both. These resources are available to eligible students whether a student applies to attend a community college, public or private college, or university. For more information about the wide variety of financial aid available, see https://studentaid.gov/understand -aid/types#grants.

Navigating the many resources available to help pay for college can be overwhelming to prospective students and their families. What is encouraging is that there are many accessible resources available for most students enrolling at community colleges. In fact, by applying for financial aid, scholarships, and grants, the cost of college may be so affordable that students have no out-of-pocket expenses. While taking advantage of these resources will require some effort to research opportunities and apply for them, the first place to start is always with the financial aid department at a local community college. A quick visit to the financial aid office website will point students and their families in the right direction for information and deadlines regarding the different types of scholarships and grants available. If needed, students may also make an appointment to meet with a financial aid staff member to receive additional help.

Free Application for Federal Student Aid (FAFSA)

The year before applying to college, students are encouraged to complete the Free Application for Federal Student Aid (FAFSA). This form is free to complete and is available online at https://studentaid.gov/h/apply-for-aid/fafsa. After completing the FAFSA form, students and their families are notified of their eligibility and access to several forms of federal financial aid, including grants, work-study, and student loans. This form may also be required to access financial aid benefits for your state of residence and community college. It is highly recommended that all students, regardless of income, complete FAFSA annually for every year the student attends college. Typically, the FAFSA form is available as early as October 1, but this can change pending the federal government's release of the annual form.

FAFSA requires details about a student and their parents' or guardians' personal information, such as name, date of birth, address, and social security number, along with information about tax and financial status. Situational information, such as citizenship or tax filing status, may necessitate certain information or documents while completing the FAFSA application. A list of all required information and documents can be found on the FAFSA website as well as helpful checklists and worksheets to help applicants gather all the necessary information to complete the form.

Various free resources and tools are available to assist with filling out the FAFSA form. These include the FAFSA website, the financial aid office at a nearby community college, and other online resources. Additionally, local events such as those held at a student's high school may be available to provide further support. To access a list of state-sponsored online resources and events aimed at helping high school students and their families learn about financial aid and find workshops, visit https://formyourfuture.org/more-resources/. As an example, Indiana provides FAFSA information and support during the state's biggest FAFSA filing event, College Goal Sunday, at https://collegegoalsunday.org/.

Promise Programs

Students are also encouraged to learn about community college promise programs. Promise programs aim to make attending community college possible by removing financial burdens. These programs are available nationwide and range from local communities to statewide initiatives. While these programs are typically community college-oriented, they may also provide benefits to attending public and private four-year institutions (Billings et al., 2021; Perna et al., 2018). Promise programs cover the cost of tuition and fees, which may provide students with free access to college or access at a significantly reduced cost (Perna et al., 2018). These programs are treated as a scholarship, which may require students to complete the FAFSA to determine the level of financial aid the promise program will provide (Billings et al., 2021; Perna et al., 2018).

Several promise programs have gained recognition and demonstrated positive impacts on broadening access to education, improving college enrollment rates, reducing financial barriers, and supporting student success. Some notable promise programs have garnered attention and praise, including Michigan's Kalamazoo Promise, the New York Excelsior Scholarship, and the Tennessee Promise. Learn more about these promise programs by visiting their websites:

◆ Kalamazoo Promise: https://www.kalamazoopromise.com/

◆ New York Excelsior Scholarship: https://www.hesc.ny
   .gov/pay-for-college/financial-aid/types-of-financial-aid
   /nys-grants-scholarships-awards/the-excelsior-scholar-
   ship.html
◆ Tennessee Promise: https://www.tn.gov/tnpromise.html

There are many ways to access information about promise programs that may be offered close to a student's home. First, College
Promise is a nonprofit organization that advocates for free community college and other promise programs. The organization
regularly maintains MyPromise at https://www.collegepromise
.org/, an online interactive map and comparison tool allowing
students to search hundreds of local and state promise programs
in the U.S. The interactive map of the U.S. allows users to search
and filter programs by state, program type, eligibility requirements, and program components. This tool provides detailed
information on each promise program listed, including program
descriptions, funding sources, application processes, and contact
information.

Second, for a comprehensive list of state financial aid offerings,
students can navigate to their state Department of Education
website for information about existing promise programs, scholarship opportunities, and other resources. State departments of
education offer accurate and reliable information about the programs available in a particular region.

Third, students can also visit community college websites in
their state of residency and search the institutions' financial aid
pages. These websites are maintained regularly and will include
information about available promise programs and application
guidelines.

Fourth, and in addition to community college websites, students can call or visit the financial aid office at their local two-
year institution to learn more about the availability of promise
programs. Financial aid staff members are knowledgeable about
the many scholarships and grant opportunities available for
their college and can be a valuable resource for students. Other
resources students may wish to explore include talking to other
students enrolled at their local community college, meeting with

their high school counselor, speaking to a college admissions representative at the institution, or attending college fairs.

Scholarships

In addition to the FAFSA, promise programs, and working with the community college's financial aid office, many scholarships are available from private and nonprofit organizations. Finding scholarship opportunities does require time and effort, but the benefits can be well worth it. Generally, it is advised that students never pay to apply for scholarships. In addition, students should be cautious of scholarships that require registration, personal information, and payment, as they may not be legitimate funding sources. Simply put, students and their families must be vigilant to avoid scams. Scholarships provide free money for tuition, school fees, books, and living expenses. Rarely will scholarships pay a student directly; instead, these resources are typically sent to the college the student is enrolled in. If excess scholarship funds remain in the student's account and the scholarship-awarding organization does not require those funds to be returned, the college will issue a refund to the student.

When applying for scholarships, keep in mind that if tuition and fees are covered by federal and state scholarships and grants, students should then focus on opportunities that will help pay for books and living expenses. Carefully read the scholarship information to decide how the awarded funds can be applied to specific financial needs. Typically, funding sources for scholarships are revealed, as are the purpose of the scholarship, the eligibility criteria, the award amount, the deadline for application, and how to apply. Application requirements may include filling out an application form, writing an essay, and obtaining letters of recommendation. Requirements will vary widely, so students should carefully follow the instructions for each scholarship opportunity applied for.

There are three primary ways to find scholarship opportunities. The first step for the student is to contact the financial aid office of the community college where they intend to apply. The financial aid office will be able to provide information about additional scholarship opportunities available through the college or through private or non-profit organizations that partner with the institution. Second, students are encouraged to search the Internet for scholarships available through the local community foundation. There are hundreds of community foundations in the U.S., which are public charities that give grants to improve local communities. A helpful tool to find community foundations can be found by using the Community Foundation Locator available at: https://cof.org/foundation-type/community-foundations. Third, a general online search for free scholarship websites can be helpful to students. According to Kumok and Hahn (2022), some popular websites to start your search include the following:

♦ Bold.com
♦ Cappex.com
♦ Careeronestop.org
♦ Collegeboard.org
♦ Fastweb.com
♦ Goingmerry.com
♦ Myscholly.com
♦ Scholarships.com
♦ Scholarshipowl.com

As another reminder, students and their families should always be diligent and keep an eye out for scams when sharing any personal information. Seek advice directly from college financial aid representatives as they are the best resources to help guide students through the complexities related to paying for college.

Student Loans

If students need additional funding after all other financial aid resources have been exhausted, borrowing money is another option available to pay for college. Experts suggest that if borrowing for college is a necessity, first borrow federal student loans before taking out private loans (Helhoski & Haverstock, 2022). Federal loans have advantages that private loans do not, such as access to income-driven repayment plans and loan forgiveness programs. As with other funding sources, students must complete the FAFSA to gain access to federal student loans.

When the financial aid package is offered at the community college the student is enrolled in, the amount and type of federal loans available to the student and their parent(s)/guardian(s) are provided at that time.

Private loans are those provided by financial institutions, such as banks, credit unions, state-based agencies, and other lenders. This type of student loan requires a comprehensive underwriting process, which includes an application process that reviews credit history and financial resources. To borrow money, lenders seek borrowers with good credit and enough disposable income to make loan payments after considering other expenses. Lenders may require students to apply with their parent(s)/guardian(s) or a co-signer who will guarantee the loan payments, to be eligible for private loans. It is essential to compare interest rates, fees, and borrower protections before choosing a lender, as many options are available (Nykiel, 2023).

Different Ways to Pay for College

There are several unique ways to pay for community college that may be worth exploring. Colleges and universities, including the community college, provide their employees with a generous payroll benefit referred to as tuition remission. With tuition remission, full-time employees, their spouses, and dependent children are typically provided with free tuition and sometimes fees and books are also covered. This is a great way for parents/guardians and their student(s) to earn college credit at the community college. To learn more about opportunities for tuition remission at the community college the student plans to attend, check the benefits section of the college's employment website or search for the college's *Staff Employment Handbook*.

Similarly, some companies offer their part-time or full-time employees tuition reimbursement or tuition assistance. With tuition reimbursement, the company reimburses the employee for education expenses as a benefit for working with them. How these programs work will depend on the company's policy, but students can generally expect to receive either a partial or full reimbursement for tuition after successfully completing a course or a semester with passing grades. To learn more about opportunities available, search the Internet for jobs that offer tuition reimbursement. Some examples of companies that offer tuition reimbursement are:

◆ Amazon, https://hiring.amazon.com/why-amazon/career-advancement/higher-education-support#/
◆ AT&T, https://www.att.jobs/benefits#tab-panel-1-2
◆ Best Buy, https://jobs.bestbuy.com/bby?id=item_detail&content=benefits
◆ Chipotle, https://jobs.chipotle.com/benefits
◆ GameStop, https://careers.gamestop.com/us/en/culture
◆ Home Depot, https://www.mythdhr.com/Benefits/Pages/TuitionReimbursement.aspx.html
◆ Lowe's, https://lowes.guildeducation.com/partner/
◆ McDonald's, https://www.archwaystoopportunity.com/tuition_assistance.html
◆ T-Mobile, https://livemagenta.com/l3/Tuition-Assistance
◆ UPS, https://www.jobs-ups.com/earn-and-learn
◆ Verizon, https://mycareer.verizon.com/life-at-verizon/benefits/
◆ Walmart, https://walmart.guildeducation.com/partner/

Another option to help cover college expenses is to participate in the Army Reserve Officers' Training Corps (ROTC). The ROTC provides scholarships to high school and college students and active-duty enlisted soldiers in exchange for service as an Army Officer after graduation. This benefit is available at certain community colleges across the U.S., which can be found by visiting the ROTC scholarship website at https://www.goarmy.com/careers-and-jobs/find-your-path/army-officers/rotc/scholarships.html.

Tax Advantages and Breaks

As we have discussed, there are a variety of ways to fund a community college education without paying for it out of pocket. However, if there are circumstances where a family may need to pay for college, advanced planning for the educational costs by saving and taking advantage of tax breaks are additional ways to reduce the cost of attending a community college. The following are some basic ways families can plan to finance their dependent's college.

Savings Plans and Accounts

Families can save for college by using tax-advantaged plans, such as 529 College Savings Plans and Coverdell Education Savings Accounts (ESA). Qualified Tuition Programs (QTP), also known as 529 College Savings Plans, are investment accounts that can be used to save for college or K-12 education (Murphy, 2022). These plans offer tax advantages, such as federal tax-deferred growth and tax-free withdrawals for qualified education expenses. Additionally, many states offer state income tax deductions or credits for contributions to a 529 plan. Many brokerage firms offer these plans.

An ESA is a tax-advantaged investment account that can be used to save for qualified education expenses of a designated beneficiary, who must be under the age of 18 when the account is opened (Kagan, 2023). An ESA and a 529 plan are similar in that they can both be used to pay for college and K-12 expenses. It is important to research all aspects of these plans and accounts before making a decision. Contribution limits, state and federal tax advantages, educational expenses covered, investment options, and fees should all be considered. For a complete understanding of tax-advantaged plans, consult with a tax professional and review the latest IRS Publication 970 for the most recent guidance available at: https://www.irs.gov/forms-pubs/about-publication-970.

Tax Credits

Currently, taxpayers who pay out of pocket for college tuition and fees for themselves, their spouse, or dependents can receive some tax relief from tax credits on their tax return. There are two tax credits that can help reduce education costs: the American Opportunity Tax Credit (AOTC) and the Lifetime Learning Credit (LLC) (Internal Revenue Service, 2022). To claim either of these credits, a taxpayer or dependent must have received a Form 1098-T from the community college, completed IRS Form 8863, and filed it with their tax return. Details about each of the credits are as follows, but we recommend students and families consult with a tax professional to understand fully how they may apply to receive these credits.

- ◆ AOTC (https://www.irs.gov/credits-deductions/individuals/aotc): The maximum benefit that can be given to each eligible student is $2,500. The credit is only valid for the first four years of undergraduate study at a college, university, or vocational school and is only available to students who are pursuing a degree or other recognized educational credential. If the tax credit reduces the tax liability to zero, the taxpayer could receive a refund of up to $1,000.

- ◆ LLC (https://www.irs.gov/credits-deductions/individuals/llc): The maximum benefit is up to $2,000 per tax return per year, regardless of the number of qualifying students. The tax credit is available for all years of undergraduate, graduate, professional degree courses, vocational school, and for courses to acquire or improve job skills. It is also available for an unlimited number of tax years.

It is important to note that these credits can be claimed on the same return but not for the same student or the same educational expenses. These credits are gradually reduced if your modified adjusted gross income is between $80,000 and $90,000 if filing as single, or $160,000 and $180,000 if filing a joint return. For more details, see https://www.eitc.irs.gov/other-refundable-credits-toolkit/compare-education-credits/compare-education-credits.

Information for International Students and Undocumented Students

For this chapter, we define international students as students who have lawfully been granted entry to study full-time in the U.S., whereas undocumented students are immigrants registered as Deferred Action on Childhood Arrivals (DACA), a federal program that allows immigrant students to lawfully reside in the U.S. without deportation. There are several advantages for international students and undocumented students who attend community college. These include, for example, improving their academic English skills, building relationships, and gaining a better understanding of U.S. culture and lifestyle. Additionally, because community colleges are an affordable option for international students to begin their studies, taking their first two years of college at the local community college results in a lower overall cost for their education (Mason, 2022).

While the options for scholarships are limited for international and undocumented students, there are some opportunities worth exploring. Like any student, non-U.S. citizens should consider contacting the financial aid office of the community college to which they intend to apply to learn about scholarship and grant opportunities. The financial aid office will be able to provide information about additional scholarship opportunities specifically available through the college, state, or through private or non-profit organizations that partner with the institution. In addition, while enrolled, international and DACA students are eligible to work at their community college.

Additional Resources for International and Undocumented Students

Below we provide some additional resources for international and undocumented students interested in the community college:

International students:

◆ *Education USA*: For a comprehensive resource on studying in the U.S. as an international student, the U.S Department of State maintains this website which includes information about events and advising centers offered internationally, including articles about the student experience and financial aid information. Website: https://educationusa.state.gov/https://educationusa.state.gov/

Non-citizens and undocumented students:

◆ *Federal Student Aid for non-citizens*: Certain groups of non-citizens qualify for federal financial aid. To learn more, visit: https://studentaid.gov/understand-aid/eligibility/requirements/non-us-citizens

- *TheDream.US*: Offers a comprehensive college access program for undocumented students with over 10,000 scholarships at over 80 colleges in more than 20 states and Washington, DC. Website: https://www.thedream.us/
- *The Golden Door Scholars*: Provides support and financial assistance to undocumented students through mentorship and community-building programs. Website: https://www.goldendoorscholars.org/
- *Immigrants Rising*: Provides undocumented students in California with resources and support for college education, careers, and mental health. Website: https://immigrantsrising.org/

Summary

Attending community college is a quality and cost-effective way to begin and obtain a degree, regardless of financial or immigration status. Students can take advantage of the various financial resources that may be necessary to earn a college degree. In this chapter, we offered an overview of the different options to help finance a community college education, including federal and state aid, scholarships, and loans, as well as tax strategies and unique opportunities. Additionally, we ended the chapter by providing international and undocumented students with information and resources to explore financial aid options for attending a community college. Remember, every student's situation is unique. As such, we do not endorse any one solution or resource provided in this chapter. Rather, we suggest all students begin with their local community college's Office of Financial Aid for accurate and timely information. Furthermore, the information shared here is subject to change.

Discussion and Reflection Prompts

Support Prompts

- What are some new ways you might help students understand and connect with resources about paying for college—and community college, in particular?

◆ Have you had conversations with students about attending college part-time while working full-time to take advantage of tuition benefits offered by employers? Why, or why not?

Student Prompts

◆ What are your thoughts about the different ways to pay for a community college education?

◆ Have you researched the cost of attending the community college of your choice? Visit https://nces.ed.gov/ipeds/collegemap/ to find out.

◆ What are your biggest concerns about financing your education?

◆ What are you doing to research and apply for scholarships and grants?

◆ Identify the companies listed in the section "Different Ways to Pay for College." Visit three websites of companies located in your community. What did you learn and how might these companies help students pay for college?

◆ How are you planning to manage your time and finances while attending college?

References

Billings, M. S., Gándara, D., & Li, A. Y. (2021). Tuition-free promise programs: Implications and lessons learned. *New Directions for Community Colleges, 2021*(196), 81–95. https://doi.org/10.1002/cc.20485

Helhoski, A., & Haverstock, E. (2022, May 25). How to pay for college: 8 tips. *Nerd Wallet*. Available at: https://www.nerdwallet.com/article/loans/student-loans/how-to-pay-for-college

Internal Revenue Service. (2022, August 11). College students should study up on these two tax credits. Available at: https://www.irs.gov/newsroom/college-students-should-study-up-on-these-two-tax-credits

Kagan, J. (2023, May 4). Coverdell education savings account (ESA): How they work. *Investopedia*. Available at: https://www.investopedia.com/terms/c/coverdellesa.asp

Kumok, Z., & Hahn, A. (2022, April 7). 9 best scholarship websites and search engines. *Forbes.* https://www.forbes.com/advisor/student-loans/best-scholarship-websites/

Ma, J., & Pender, M. (2023). *Trends in college pricing and student aid 2023.* College Board. Available at: https://research.collegeboard.org/media/pdf/Trends%20Report%202023%20Updated.pdf

Mason, L. (2022). *Welcoming international students at U.S. community colleges.* Available at: AIFS/IIE Global Education Research Report Series. Institute of International Education. https://www.iie.org/wp-content/uploads/2022/12/AIFS_IIE_WelcomingIntenrationalStudentsatU.S.CommunityColleges_2022_FINAL_web.pdf

Murphy, R. (2022, July 2). How to start a 529 plan. *Investopedia.* Available at: https://www.investopedia.com/how-to-start-529-plan-5496586

Nykiel, T. (2023, August 3). How to apply for student loans: Federal and private. *Nerd Wallet.* Available at: https://www.nerdwallet.com/article/loans/student-loans/student-loans-federal-vs-private-loans

Perna, L. W., Leigh, E. W., & Carroll, S. (2018). "Free college": A new and improved state approach to increasing educational attainment? *American Behavioral Scientist, 61*(14), 1740–1756. https://doi.org/10.1177/0002764217744821

7

Student and Campus Life

While most may think of the classroom as located within a brick-and-mortar physical space, it is important to reconsider this paradigm when discussing contemporary community colleges. In fact, these places of discovery—*classrooms*—can be found in an online learning environment, either virtually in real time (synchronous) or asynchronously where students and faculty engage online but at different times. Internships offer meaningful learning opportunities for students, and *classrooms* may be incubators or laboratories located off-campus at a local industry or business. Additionally, hybrid learning combines multiple classroom modalities, which may include a mix of face-to-face on-campus, virtual, and asynchronous online learning. To be clear, our concept of *classroom* must be expanded to include all modalities of learning available to today's community college students. In this chapter, we further emphasize what we have discussed throughout the book—that the community college is nimble in terms of meeting the learning needs of diverse student populations.

The community college classroom must be thought of broadly. Some might argue learning can happen in any space, and not just in classrooms. In fact, might basketball courts, green spaces, and community study rooms also be *classrooms*? To be sure, the cornerstone of any college education is the magic that happens in the classroom. Here is where students engage with talented faculty and peers, sharing their views about ideas and working together to understand new concepts and skills. College

DOI: 10.4324/9781003346210-7

classrooms, however defined, stimulate curiosity and can be the conduit for new ways of thinking, often leading to lifetime passions and heightened career interests. At the same time, there are *so many* ways college students learn outside and beyond the formal college curriculum.

In this chapter, we also provide an overview of student and campus life in diverse community college settings. Regardless of their location or size, community colleges offer activities, services, and resources meant to complement the institution's academic mission and support student success and retention. These may include new student orientations, academic advising, career development and education, disability services, financial aid, health and wellness, tutoring, study abroad, and cultural centers. Also, in this chapter, we discuss how community colleges promote student progression to completion (graduation) and a sense of belonging through physical spaces, faculty and peer relationships, college support systems, and community engagement opportunities.

As educators, we understand that much learning occurs outside of our classrooms, however defined, yet still within the institution. This learning is often what higher education practitioners refer to as the co-curriculum—all that students learn throughout a college experience outside the formal academic curriculum—which often happens through *student life* and/or *campus life*. Many students choose to get involved in activities through student/campus life, such as athletics, social and academic clubs, organizations with community ties, and campus events. The range of what is available in terms of student/campus life varies, however, by institution type. And while there will likely be fewer student life activities available to students attending a non-residential two-year college than at a residential four-year institution, this does not mean community college students have nothing to do on campus outside of the formal classroom. In fact, student affairs offices at community colleges are robust where staff work hard to ensure students have meaningful opportunities to engage actively with the institution, college personnel, their fellow students, and, in some cases, with the outside community.

The assortment of on-campus activities and resources among community colleges is striking. Some community college campuses resemble a four-year residential college, complete with on-campus housing and vibrant residence life programming; on-campus dining options; sprawling student centers with meeting rooms, study areas, and a bustling bookstore; and a well-resourced library. Other institutions may have smaller campus facilities with fewer offices and streamlined departments. Community colleges often have satellite campus locations in addition to their primary campus. These auxiliary campuses may be found in locations such as strip malls, converted grocery stores, former car dealerships, historic buildings, and other unexpected places. While satellite campuses may *feel* different than their main campuses, many services and activities will still be available to students. Remember, community colleges seek to meet the needs of all students, which means accessible, closer to home, and so on.

Belonging in (Community) College

Students thrive in college—and graduate—for many reasons. Often, a sense of belonging is at the heart of these reasons (Strayhorn, 2019). It is important for students to feel included and connected to their college, other students, and faculty (Ahn & Davis, 2020). Feelings and attitudes such as social acceptance, affirmation, and self-confidence can positively impact students as they journey through their college careers. As innately social creatures, human beings have a strong need to feel a sense of belonging. It feels good to belong and be accepted by others. College students, regardless of age or background, are no exception. Higher education leaders and administrators understand this well and are eager to intentionally create ways for students to be connected to, integrated into, involved with, and engaged within the institution. A sense of belonging is integral to student success, as students who feel like they belong tend to be more successful in college. If students feel like they belong, they are more likely to persist toward completion. There has been much research on the topics of student persistence and institutional retention, going back decades (Habley et al., 2011; Reason & Braxton, 2023; Tinto, 1975, 1993).

This connection between a student's sense of belonging and their overall collegiate success matters a great deal to postsecondary institutions. Student persistence and completion help fulfill the institution's mission. Institutions can cultivate a culture of belonging, but it must be done with intentionality. For example, a culture of belonging must be cultivated on campus within physical classrooms, offices and departments, common campus spaces, as well as in the online learning environment. Further, marketing campaigns and institutional websites must be crafted with institutional messaging and branding that are inclusive to all—students, staff, faculty, and others. Just a few examples of on-campus inclusive spaces that promote a sense of belonging include lactation rooms, gender-expansive bathrooms, and classroom furniture that is comfortable for all body sizes and physical abilities. Students who may assume a community college cannot welcome them fully, and in ways that a four-year institution can, really should think again. A quick visit to any community college campus and/or their website should put this concern to rest.

Spaces and Places

The lines between home, school, and work have become increasingly blurred, particularly after the lockdown resulting from COVID-19. In fact, many more Americans are choosing to work remotely, and some employers are seeing the advantages of reduced office space costs as they allow employees to spend all/ some of their time working from home. Educators face many of the same considerations as well, as more and more students are *doing* college from home and away from brick-and-mortar campuses. While online education, virtual meetings, and remote work were growing before the pandemic, the growth following it has been significant. Colleges and universities that were hesitant to enter the e-learning space before 2020 today continue to offer online learning options to their students. Community colleges were early adopters of this modality, but in many cases they too have increased their online options to ensure maximum access for students. Regardless of where students choose to attend college, we understand that facilities and space (physical/ remote) utilization impact students' overall college experience and learning.

As noted earlier, community college administrators offer some of the most innovative solutions in terms of where to offer classes and how to best serve students. In some cases, revitalized buildings are converted into classrooms and computer labs. In other examples, students attend community college classes in retrofitted mall storefronts or in former public school buildings. The diversity of physical places and spaces often matches the diversity of students within these spaces, thus, complementing a student's rich learning experience. In considering these spaces/places of learning, it is important to understand the student experience and what meanings students derive from these experiences. Simply put, whether the learning spaces have new furniture or cutting-edge technologies, what matters most is that they are designed for learning and inquiry and invoke a sense of belonging where students are inspired to share ideas and collaborate with others—or to learn.

Academic Spaces and Places
Classrooms

Community colleges often offer smaller class sizes than do large four-year colleges and universities. First-year students on major university campuses can expect to attend classes in large lecture halls that accommodate several hundred students. Not only can large class sizes be less favorable for learning, but they can also be a challenge for faculty to manage. While the average class size at community colleges is around 25 to 30 students (Kisker et al., 2023), many universities have freshman classes with hundreds of enrolled students. Not every student struggles in larger classes, but some do. Generally, smaller class size translates to more personal interaction with the instructor and a greater opportunity to meet and interact with peers, leading to a stronger sense of belonging and connection. Smaller class sizes can facilitate dialogue and community where students are able to gain a better understanding of culture, experiences, and beliefs that differ from their own.

As highlighted throughout this book, community colleges serve many different student populations and access is at the core of their mission. Diversity is defined widely and includes race, ethnicity, learning differences, abilities, sexual orientation, and age. This is not meant to be an exhaustive list. While we know that college in general expands students' ideas around culture and identity, we also believe that community colleges may be uniquely equipped to serve the disparate groups of learners they attract. We also know that learning goes far beyond books and lectures. In diverse community college classrooms, whether virtual or on campus, students benefit in terms of increased cultural awareness, exposure to varied viewpoints, and new ways of thinking. It is well documented that all students benefit from being part of diverse classrooms and learning environments.

Faculty Offices

As stated previously (see Chapter 5), community college faculty are vital to the educational lives of community college students (Schudde, 2019). In this chapter, we include faculty offices as important places of learning for students. Community college faculty are typically required to hold office hours to meet with students where they answer questions and provide insight into their field or discipline. High achieving students can particularly benefit from meeting with their faculty members to discuss topics more deeply as they relate to their interests and aspirations. In some cases, faculty provide support for research projects and presentations outside of course assignments where high achieving students seek to showcase their work (Hensel, 2021). Creating these relationships with faculty is also important to students who will need a letter of recommendation from a faculty member at some point in their academic journey. Such professional relationships can last well beyond a student's two-year education.

Libraries

Like the classroom, libraries are important learning spaces for college students and others. And although community college libraries may be smaller than those found at four-year institutions, their importance to students, faculty, and community members who visit the library must not be underestimated. Today, libraries may be shared spaces with tutoring centers or other student support offices, but they do exist at every accredited community college. In fact, accrediting bodies require students to have access to libraries and learning resource centers. For some people, the idea of a library conjures up images of quiet spaces with stacks of dusty books and a librarian shushing/quieting everyone who enters. This is no longer the case in community college libraries, which have evolved into global resource repositories, gathering places, and collaborative workspaces.

Community college libraries meet the unique needs of learners. For example, commuter students may use the library to finish assignments while they are waiting between classes. Students without home computers often utilize the library's computers to complete research papers and other homework. The library is often where students meet with peers to study and collaborate. Today's community college campus library is electronically connected to thousands of research documents through shared interlibrary loan programs and vast online subscriptions such as EbscoHost and ProQuest, which host countless resources for the campus community to access for free. In addition to providing free Internet connection to students and guests, community college libraries typically offer students access to printers and textbooks, should they be unable to buy their texts prior to the start of the semester. The duties of library staff members have also changed over time. While their work has evolved mostly because of advances in technology and information literacy, these community college employees remain an important frontline resource for students, faculty, and others.

Because most community colleges do not have residence halls/dorms, college administrators and space planners are intentional in creating gathering, resting, and study spaces for the commuter student population. In many cases, it is the campus library that offers important collaborative workspaces for students with access to computers and enhanced technology. Often study rooms in the library can be reserved and students and other guests may have access to free coffee and other snacks to encourage their visits to the library. Additionally, some community colleges have relocated their tutoring centers and other academic support services to the library area. And while libraries continue to house books and other bound materials, in most cases, their physical footprint is decreasing because of the availability of—and demand for—online materials. Online resources are especially important for students who cannot travel easily to campus such as working adults, students living in rural areas, and students without access to transportation.

Non-Academic Spaces and Places
Student Centers

The Student Center, sometimes known as a Student Union or Student Commons, can be a *hub* for student engagement. In today's student centers, we find the intersection of technology and human interaction where students can connect socially and have access to resources for academic and career success. In these centers, students congregate and make important social connections with their peers. With diverse community college students meeting in such common areas, these spaces help students build interpersonal and collaborative skills. Typically, these centers are not as large as what is found on four-year college campuses, but they could be. Many two-year student centers include coffee shops, lounges, food courts, meeting rooms, and vending machines. Often, campus bookstores are located in student centers as well. Historically, these commons spaces have also served as key college recruitment and retention spaces. Campus tours for prospective students and guests often start and end in student centers. Additionally, these spaces serve an important marketing role as visitors get a sense of the institution's brand within these spaces. Facilities planners, at two- and four-year institutions alike, seek to make these and other common areas safe places where students feel a sense of belonging and attachment to their peers and college in general.

Cultural Centers

Like four-year institutions, many community colleges offer cultural centers. These important centers offer a safe, comfortable, and educational space for specific identity-based groups and the broader campus community. Simply put, these centers are critical for belongingness among marginalized and minoritized groups. For example, it is common for higher education institutions to house a women's center, a Black cultural center, and/or an LGBTQ+ center. These physical campus locations provide spaces for students to gather, dedicated staff, access to specific resources, and educational programming. For example, Lane Community College in Oregon has a Gender Equity Center. See https://www.lanecc.edu/get-support/resource-centers/gender -equity-center. The existence and creation of such centers are typically based on the student population. An influx of a specific population to a particular geographic area may be one reason to start such a center. One example might be an increase in a particular refugee population, which could suggest the need for a cultural center specific to the group's culture, religion, and so on.

On-Campus Housing

While it may seem counterintuitive, some community colleges do offer on-campus housing. In fact, around 29% of community colleges nationwide have some sort of on-campus housing available for students (AACC, 2023). On-campus housing is more likely to be available to rural community college students who may have long commutes to campus. Additionally, institutions with a significant number of student-athletes and/or international students may also offer housing. Often, these accommodations are available to traditional-aged college students (aged 18–24) who are not married and who do not have children and/ or older students who may have families. Some housing is akin to a traditional four-year residence hall with two-person rooms along a hallway or organized in suites with common restrooms and kitchens and/or lounges for an entire floor or suite, while other student housing is apartment-style with several bedrooms and common greenspaces that may also include a playground for children. Some institutions own and manage their on-campus housing, while others contract with outside entities to provide a wide variety of housing options.

Recreation Centers

Leisure and recreational activities often lead to social interaction, which can also help community college students build relationships with their peers. Community colleges offer a wide variety of recreational spaces. Smaller urban campuses may have very limited or no recreational space available to students, whereas large community college campuses may include soccer fields, bowling alleys, swimming pools, and running tracks, among many other options. Some community colleges have intramural and club sports as well, which provide great opportunities for students to get involved, gain school pride, and make new friends. For some students, opportunities such as these are unimportant, yet to others, such affordances and activities are seen as a priority to their enrollment. Campus recreational facilities such as gymnasiums and swimming pools may be available to the local community for a yearly or monthly fee, which generates additional income for the community college. This can be a great way to give back to the community, especially for colleges that rely on local property taxes, levies, and millages for operating support. Additional examples include cardio and weightlifting equipment, group fitness classes, pickleball courts, and yoga studios.

Performing Arts

As we have discussed throughout this book, two-year institutions serve not only enrolled students but also their community at large. With a community-focused organizational mission, community colleges are often cultural hubs for area residents and lifelong learners. As such, many of their facilities and common spaces are shared among students and community members. By sharing these spaces, institutions further help build identity and belonging which can benefit all who visit their campus(es). At schools with theater and dance programs, for example, spaces for classes, rehearsals, and student-led productions may also be open to the community for use. Professional artists seeking a venue may find availability at the local community college. Like recreational facilities, additional revenue can be generated by renting such spaces, though they could be available to the public at no cost. Theaters and auditoriums are often used as spaces to gather large numbers of students to celebrate student successes. For example, institution-wide graduation ceremonies or awards events often utilize auditoriums or theater spaces. Again, congregation areas such as these can help promote a sense of belonging, achievement, and pride among students, faculty and staff, and the wider community.

Outdoor Spaces

Many colleges create outdoor green spaces to encourage further recreational opportunities and places for students to connect. With student mental health a growing concern among educators, community colleges are considering how they might include more green spaces in their facilities planning. Campus green spaces can lead to reduced depression, reduced stress, and improved mental health (Liu et al., 2022). These spaces may include a small brick courtyard with benches or a fully landscaped rolling lawn with bike paths where students can study, relax, or hang out with friends. And as with other common areas, green spaces can help build a sense of belonging and community among students. Some urban colleges go a step further and provide communal gardens to help students with food insecurity or provide educational opportunities for students. One example is the Inver Hills Community Garden & Orchard in Inver Grove Heights, Minnesota. This is a cooperative learning opportunity between Inver Hills Community College students, community members, faculty, and staff. It includes a 1-acre garden, an apple orchard, and outdoor seating space for classes and speakers (Inver Hills News, 2021). These innovative spaces provide great links between communities and students with interactive networking possibilities. Deemed by some as one of the nation's most beautiful community college campuses is Fond du Lac Tribal & Community College. To learn more about the natural beauty available to its students and visitors, see https://fdltcc .edu/about-us/campus/.

Campus Units and Student Activities

Athletics
For students seeking to participate in collegiate athletics, the community college may be just the right fit. Community colleges with athletic departments and sports teams are sanctioned by the National Junior College Athletics Association (NJCAA). The NJCAA serves as the national governing body for two-year college athletics in the U.S. and is the nation's second-largest national intercollegiate sports organization (second to the NCAA). Each year, over 60,000 student-athletes from over 500 member colleges compete in 28 different sports. In addition, the NJCAA hosts more than 50 national championship events each year (see https://www.njcaa.org/championships/landing/index). The availability of competitive athletics varies greatly from region to region and state to state. Regardless, many community colleges boast robust and successful athletic programs in a wide variety of men's and women's sports, including tennis, football, basketball, softball, wrestling, golf, and bowling. Some students may see participation in an NJCAA team as a vehicle for eventually transferring into an NCAA Division I program, while others may see it as a healthy and enriching complement to their community college experience. Student athletes who begin at a two-year institution will save a great deal of money while advancing in their sport and earning college credits that transfer.

Student Clubs
Student organizations offer many opportunities for students to learn and develop new skills, such as leadership and communication. All community colleges have a variety of student clubs

available on their campuses. Students who actively participate in college clubs and organizations often speak about the networks and friendships they make, some of which last a lifetime. Additionally, at some institutions, community service clubs link students with the local community through meaningful service project opportunities. Participating in a student club can enhance a student's experience at the community college while also serving to build their resume. Students—regardless of their abilities or major—who are active on campus demonstrate initiative and interest in developing leadership skills which is important to employers and admissions representatives at four-year institutions.

Global Education and Travel Abroad

If you thought travel abroad experiences were only offered at a four-year institution, think again. Not only are community college students traveling across the globe, in some cases they may have extended opportunities to study overseas. In one example, Northern Community College in Virginia (NOVA) offers study abroad opportunities in Korea, the Czech Republic, and Scotland. Additionally, NOVA students can apply for a scholarship to help fund their study abroad. To learn more, visit https://www .nvcc.edu/about/offices/international-education/study-abroad .html. The Community Colleges for International Development organization also offers scholarships to college students who study abroad. Information regarding this resource can be found at https://www.ccidinc.org/study-abroad-scholarships/. As we think about community college students as global citizens, study and/or travel abroad can provide a rich experience for students to gain cultural competencies. Four-year colleges and universities do not have a monopoly on these important experiential activities.

On-Campus, Near-Campus, and Online Student Services and Resources

Clearly, student activities and student services at community colleges are prolific and ever-changing to meet the needs of learners. Today, many critical student services are offered on campuses as well as remotely. While we focus on a limited number of student services here, it is important to understand that your local community college likely offers many more services and resources than we can highlight in this chapter.

New Student Orientation

Before starting college, most institutions offer, and in many cases require, orientation programming for new students. Community colleges are no exception. College orientation is often the first time students meet and feel that they too belong in college. Activities in orientation may include taking a campus tour, being introduced to campus resources, ensuring access to campus technology and systems, learning about campus policies, getting a student identification card, and meeting with academic advisors. Some examples of campus resources commonly highlighted during orientation include the library, health services, counseling center, campus food pantry, and tutoring services. Understanding the technology students need to be successful in college can be especially daunting for new students. As such, orientation helps students better understand and set up access to their college email, cloud storage, learning management systems, campus-specific apps, course registration, library databases, and online access to bill pay. Many important campus policies are typically memorialized in a student handbook and shared with students during orientations. Relevant policies addressed may include academic integrity, the use of substances like tobacco on campus, parking rules and regulations, bias incident reporting, library fees, online netiquette, and account holds. As a new student, navigating college systems and resources can be overwhelming. Orientations seek to acclimate students to help make the first weeks of college smoother. The use of interactive online orientations at community colleges is growing as well and may include assessment tests that students take after completing orientation.

Academic Advising

A critical student service at the community college is academic advising. In fact, many studies point to academic advising as one of the most important functions related to student success.

In some cases, students will work with an advisor in the advising center, while in other instances they will be directed to a faculty advisor. Most two-year institutions have professional advisors who are full-time staff members and whose primary responsibility is to advise students. Advising is more than scheduling classes. According to the National Academic Advising Association (NACADA), advising equates to teaching as it involves conversation around career interests and transfer goals. At some institutions, *college counselor* denotes college staff members who provide academic advising, career education, and mental health counseling. And in some cases, individuals in these positions can earn tenure, like some full-time faculty members. Academic advisors help ensure students register for classes that fit with their work and family schedules, count toward credential completion, and help them reach their ultimate goals which may include transferring to a four-year institution. Academic advisors play an important role in student development by helping students make good decisions, learn how to ask for help when they need it, communicate with faculty, and increase their level of confidence. Every community college will provide access to an advisor or counselor, but students must remember it is a shared responsibility in terms of their success. Students should be proactive and reach out to their advisor rather than wait passively to receive information or support. Additionally, students should enter every advising appointment prepared with ideas about their goals and with a list of questions to make good use of their time together.

Financial Aid

The financial aid office is a vital resource for any college student. For new and prospective students, these offices can help with the Free Application for Federal Student Aid (FAFSA). Some community colleges have centralized their financial aid services to better process applications and serve students in a timelier manner. The Financial Aid Office is the hub for applying for and receiving financial aid through loans, grants, scholarships, and other sources. Students likely will receive a great deal of communication from their financial aid office. Questions related to tuition and statements can be addressed by staff members in these offices. Financial aid specialists can also help students navigate applying for scholarships and grants, including those available only to certain student populations. Veteran and military tuition benefits are available as well as employer tuition assistance programs. Staff in community college financial aid offices understand these assistance programs and can help students develop a funding plan to help pay for college tuition and other costs. Additionally, Federal Work-Study programs are managed by the Office of Financial Aid. FAFSA eligible students may consider participating in the work-study program where they receive tuition assistance in return for working part-time at the college. Positions can vary throughout the institution and may include clerical roles, food service, or library positions. There are many nuances to financial aid that vary by institution. States may offer resources to students to help scale the local employee economy by providing financial support for specific certificate or degree programs. And while the cost of attending community colleges is lower than the cost of attending a four-year university, with help from the financial aid office, these costs may be even further reduced. See Chapter 6 for an in-depth look at paying for college.

Tutoring Centers

Visiting the institution's tutoring center for academic help, whether on campus or remote, is a great idea for most students. Many community colleges offer free tutoring in a variety of subjects, such as math and English. While there is typically a focus on these two critical subjects, tutoring in other disciplines such as history, psychology, and anatomy and physiology may also be available. Students will be reminded of tutoring services and hours during their orientation program. Faculty and staff members may serve as tutors and in some cases, full-time tutors are hired to serve students. As stated previously, libraries are now home to many community college tutoring centers.

Parking, Campus Shuttles, Public Transportation Discounts

Community colleges are often referred to as *commuter schools* as so many students drive or take public transportation to campus.

As such, community colleges typically have large parking lots to accommodate commuter students. These parking lots are usually well-lit, and many have security presence for students walking to their cars after attending an evening class or campus event. Larger campuses may offer campus or city-wide free shuttle services to assist students. Additionally, many communities partner with colleges to offer free bus shuttle programs for students with valid IDs.

On-Campus Technology

Community colleges offer access to on-campus technology in a variety of ways. At minimum, institutions offer Internet, computers, and printers for student use. These resources may be located in the library or in a centrally located place such as the Student Center. Some students may not have Internet connectivity at home, so these campus resources are critical to their ability to attend college and complete coursework. Additional technology may be campus-specific based on the degree or certification offerings at that campus. For example, community colleges offering a robotics degree may have state-of-the-art robotic equipment for students to use in a laboratory. Also, nursing, surgery technology, and emergency management programs may provide a variety of technologies to enable simulations. Often this teaching and laboratory equipment has been donated by a local employer seeking to gain a well-trained workforce through a partnership with the community college. This is a win-win-win for the college, employers, and future employees—also known as community college graduates.

Testing Centers/Services

As highlighted in previous chapters, community colleges are open-access institutions, which means anyone can benefit from the affordances of higher education through their local community college. While many community college students are placed in college-level courses via high school GPAs, in some cases, they will need to take an assessment/test for placement purposes. Admissions representatives can direct prospective community college students to the testing center when needed. All prospective students will be required to submit a high school diploma or equivalent credential (GED) though these documents do not always have to be submitted immediately in the matriculation process.

When needed, assessment typically occurs in three areas: math, reading, and writing. Many administer ACCUPLACER (see https://accuplacer.collegeboard.org/) at no cost to students. Here is an example of a City Colleges of Chicago's placement testing website, which includes relevant institutional policies: https://www.ccc.edu/services/Pages/Placement-Tests.aspx. Prior learning assessment (PLA) is another way community colleges place students in appropriate classes and award credit for work experience which may include licensure and certifications that can be cross-walked to college credit. Ivy Tech Community College in Indiana has a robust PLA website: https://www/ivy-tech.edu/admissions/credit-for-prior-learing/. The College Level Examination Program (CLEP) is another avenue students can take to earn college credit via assessment rather than enrollment in a course. DANTES Standardized Subject Tests (DSST) is available to U.S. military members, including those in the National Guard, Reserves, and the U.S. Coast Guard. Finally, community colleges offer testing services necessary for completing industry credentials, certifications, and licensure. Students interested in Automotive Service Excellence (ASE) certification, for example, may be able to sit for the certification exams at their local community college's Testing Center. Testing and assessment information including any required fees is available on every community college website.

Mental Health and Addiction Recovery Resources

Community college student mental health is a topic gaining much attention (Latz, 2023). Many community colleges offer on-campus counseling centers or access to on-campus mental health counseling and support. In cases where this is not available, faculty and staff members are typically able to connect students with resources available within the local community. Other ways community colleges support student mental health is through an emphasis on care and implementing *Caring*

Campus initiatives (for more information, see https://www.iebc-now.org/caring-campus/). Some community colleges have created CARE Centers to support students. In the case of North Hennepin Community College in Minnesota, CARE stands for Counseling, Advocacy, Resources, and Empowerment, but this naming convention is not universal. See https://www.nhcc.edu/student-resources/counseling-and-basic-needs. Community colleges have also brought social workers onto the staff, connected students to tele-health services specifically for mental health care, and added dedicated spaces to campus meant to promote mindfulness and a sense of calm such as Gateway Community College's Serenity Room: https://www.gatewaycc.edu/students/diversiy-equity-inclusion/serenity-room at its Washington campus in Phoenix, Arizona.

Similarly, collegiate recovery programs are meant to support students with substance abuse disorder. Collegiate recovery programs are becoming more prevalent in the face of the nation's ongoing opioid epidemic. Opioids include heroin, fentanyl, and oxycodone. More information about these programs can be found at the Association of Recovery in Higher Education's website at https://collegiaterecovery.org/. Not only do these programs support students, but they also create the infrastructure needed to educate the campus community regarding this important issue. Because knowledge can be life-saving, many campuses also provide college-wide training for the administration of naloxone, one of the medications used to reverse an opioid overdose.

Childcare Services

Single parenting students comprise 16% of the community college student population (AACC, 2023). While not every community college offers childcare services on campus, doing so can make a significant difference to students' ability to attend class, study, and participate in campus events. In short, finding quality and reliable childcare can make the difference between college retention and attrition for parenting students. When on-campus childcare is not available, some institutions offer support in the form of referrals and vouchers. Furthermore, students can be supported through parenting training, workshops, and other resources. Salt Lake City Community College's Childcare and Family Services website offers examples. See https://www.slcc .edu/childcare/index.aspx.

Disability Services

Many students with disabilities and learning differences have not only the ability to thrive in college but also the desire to do so. Approximately 21% of community college students have a diagnosed and disclosed disability (AACC, 2023). These disabilities may be visible or invisible. One example of a visible disability is someone who uses a wheelchair or powerchair to move across campus. Examples of invisible disabilities may include vision or hearing impairments, autism, and learning challenges such as ADHD. To comply with the Americans with Disabilities Act (ADA), community colleges must provide disabled students with reasonable accommodations such that access to educational opportunities is equitable. In the case of someone with a mobility disability, accommodations may include ramps and curb cuts within walkways and elevators inside multi-story buildings for a chair user. In the case of students with learning disabilities, accommodations such as use of a voice recorder to capture lectures, an assigned scribe, or additional time to complete tests, quizzes, or assignments are among standard accommodations provided by colleges. Disability services offices are a vital resource for students to access higher education. Further, federal law requires community colleges to meet the needs of students with documented disabilities. Personnel in disability offices regularly meet and work with students concerning the nature of their disability. They also work alongside students to decide on reasonable accommodations that neither infringe on the integrity of student learning nor the learning goals associated with the course. In addition, disability services provide ongoing training and professional development for faculty and others who work directly with students with disabilities. Faculty are often introduced to Universal Design for Learning (UDL), where educators design their courses and course materials to be accessible to all. An example of UDL includes captioning in all course videos, even when no students in the course are known to be deaf or hearing impaired. Another example is ensuring all course documents are legible to screen reading software. To learn more about UDL, visit https://universaldesign.ie/about-universal-design

It is important that students with disabilities advocate for themselves when they enter college. In some cases, the transition from high school to college can be challenging because of the increased need to self-advocate. It is incumbent upon students to meet with disability services if they wish to receive accommodations. This conferral will involve providing paperwork where the disability/ies are documented. Documentation may come from the student's medical doctor, mental health care provider, or educational psychologist. Disability services will provide students with accommodation letters (often electronic) to share with their faculty or the documents will be sent directly to the students' faculty member(s). This service is vital to equitable access to higher education for community college students with disabilities.

Veterans Services

Veterans comprise approximately 5% of the community college student population (AACC, 2023). This student population, like many others, has unique needs and expectations for their college experience. For example, veterans may be navigating GI Bill benefits as well as managing culture shock/shifts. These students may also desire a regimented schedule and one with strict routines and a clear hierarchy. Student veterans may have post-traumatic stress and need resources and support in managing their stress in healthy ways. The Center for Military & Veterans Education at Tidewater Community College in Virginia offers a great example of what a community college can offer students in active duty, student veterans, and their families. See https://www.tcc.edu/service-support/military/. Many community colleges are *military friendly* and provide a high-level of support for this population of students, including designated staff to assist students who are active in or veterans of the U.S. Armed Forces. Learn more about and compare GI Bill benefits at approved institutions here: https://www.va.gov/education/gi-bill-comparison-tool/.

Summary

In this chapter we focused on student and campus life at the community college which enriches the two-year experience. Additionally, we highlighted student services and resources that may be available on- and off-campus which aid in student retention and success. After reading this chapter, prospective students and their families may be surprised to learn that such a variety of supports and experiential opportunities such as study/travel abroad are available to community college students. In many cases, these offerings and opportunities are on par with those offered at four-year colleges and universities. Though most community colleges are considered commuter schools, some institutions do in fact offer on-campus housing to their students. To help students feel a sense of belonging, a great deal of planning and improvements has been made to community college campuses (both inside and outside) to ensure public and private spaces across campus are welcoming and conducive to community-building, collaboration, and learning. We emphasized how inclusion and belonging on campus matter to both students and institutions and some of the steps community colleges across the U.S. are taking to ensure greater inclusion. We also emphasized how spaces and places—academic and non-academic—are designed and made available to students and the broader community to promote community, relaxation, and overall improved physical and mental health of students and visitors. Further, we discussed how these places and spaces represent the college's branding which embodies institutional values and culture. Finally, we focused on critical campus services and resources, such as offices of financial aid, advising, and disability services, which exist to support every type and population of learner. Certainly, these and many other services are available on your local community college campus.

Discussion and Reflection Prompts

Support Prompts

- ◆ Before reading this chapter, were you aware of the many resources community colleges have to offer? Why, or why not? What has contributed to your level of awareness?

- What surprised you most about this chapter?
- Does your local community college offer any resources or services not included in this chapter? If yes, how can you learn more?

Student Prompts

- Of the elements of campus life and resources shared here, what are you most interested in learning more about? What are some ways you can learn more?
- Going to college can mean more than just going to classes. Brainstorm the potential benefits of college engagement beyond coursework. Here are three examples to get you started: making friends, developing leadership skills, and growing confidence.

References

AACC (American Association of Community Colleges). (2023). *Fast facts*. Available at: https://www.aacc.nche.edu/research-trends/fast-facts/

Ahn, M. Y., & Davis, H. H. (2020). Four domains of students' sense of belonging to university. *Studies in Higher Education, 45*(3), 622–634. https://doi.org/10.1080/03075079.2018.1564902

Habley, W. R., Bloom, J. L., & Robbins, S. (2011). *Increasing persistence: Research-based strategies for college student success.* Wiley.

Hensel, N. H. (2021). *Undergraduate research at community colleges: Equity, discovery, and innovation.* Stylus.

Inver Hills News. (2021, March 24). Inver community garden & orchard. Blog. Available at: https://news.inverhills.edu/blog/inver-hills-community-garden-orchard-spring-2021/

Kisker, C. B., Cohen, A. M., & Brawer, F. B. (2023). *The American community college* (7th ed.). Wiley.

Latz, A. O. (2023). *Community college student mental health: Faculty experiences and institutional actions.* Rowman & Littlefield.

Liu, W., Sun, N., Guo, J., & Zheng, Z. (2022). Campus green spaces, academic achievement and mental health of college students. *International Journal of Environmental Research and Public Health, 19*(14), 8618. https://doi.org/10.3390/ijerph19148618

Reason, R. D., & Braxton, J. M. (Eds.). (2023). *Improving college student retention: New developments in theory, research, and practice.* Routledge.

Schudde, L. (2019). Short- and long-term impacts of engagement experiences with faculty and peers at community colleges. *The Review of Higher Education, 42*(2), 385–426. https://doi.org/10.1353/rhe.2019.0001

Strayhorn, T. L. (2019). *College students' sense of belonging: A key to educational success for all students* (2nd ed.). Routledge.

Tinto, V. (1975). Dropout from higher education: A theoretical synthesis of recent research. *Review of Educational Research, 45*(1), 89–125. https://doi.org/10.2307/1170024

Tinto, V. (1993). *Leaving college: Rethinking the causes and cures of student attrition* (2nd ed.). University of Chicago Press.

8

Technology and the Post-Pandemic Community College

Since the Great Recession, nothing has impacted higher education more than the COVID-19 pandemic. However, because of their agility, community colleges were able to pivot quickly to online and virtual teaching and learning. While this flexibility provided continuity for students, community colleges are still overcoming significant disruptions caused by the global pandemic, including enrollment decreases and changes in general enrollment patterns. More than anything, though, the pandemic accelerated efforts by community colleges to manage and improve operations to survive amidst the chaos of COVID-19 and ultimately provide better learning experiences for their students, becoming more attuned to students' ever-changing circumstances and needs.

In this chapter, we highlight the various technologies and tools, such as Artificial Intelligence (AI) and Learning Management Systems (LMSs), that community colleges use to provide services and instruction to diverse student populations. The pandemic certainly forced all institutions of higher education to grow in terms of virtual and distance learning, supported by various forms of technology. Yet community colleges have always been willing and able to experiment with new and innovative ways to provide learning experiences to their students. Here, we provide a general overview of the

DOI: 10.4324/9781003346210-8

growing interest in online learning at the community college, which started long before COVID-19, and describe synchronous and asynchronous learning modalities. A student testimonial is shared to illustrate further how online learning works well for community college students. Big Tech's interest in partnering with community colleges to help train and hire future employees in cybersecurity and other high-need areas is also briefly addressed in this chapter. In addition, we discuss some hidden costs of attending college, such as technology and online course fees. Finally, we close the chapter by discussing how community colleges are increasing their focus on supporting student mental health post-COVID-19.

COVID-19 Impacts on Community Colleges

The Coronavirus Aid, Relief, and Economic Security Act, or CARES Act, was passed by Congress on March 27, 2020. This bill allotted $2.2 trillion to provide fast and direct economic aid to the American people negatively impacted by the COVID-19 pandemic. Approximately $14 billion was given to the Office of Postsecondary Education as the Higher Education Emergency Relief Fund, or HEERF (see https://www2.ed.gov/about/offices/list/ope/caresact.html). The CARES Act was an economic stimulus bill that provided $2.2 trillion in aid, including approximately "$300 billion in one-time payments to individuals, $260 billion in unemployment benefits, and $339.8 billion in aid to state and local governments" (Bray, 2021, p. 3).

Of the $339.8 billion in relief funds (Bray, 2021, p. 3), $13 billion was awarded to K-12 education and $14 billion to higher education (Snell, 2020). These dollars were critical to community colleges as they could assist students who needed access to technology services, Internet access, and computers to ensure they could remain enrolled in classes, all of which were abruptly offered only online due to the pandemic. For example, many community colleges loaned laptops and personal hotspots to students who attended college from home during the pandemic. In another example, it was not uncommon during this time for students across the nation to drive to campus parking lots to access the Internet so they could persist with their studies. Navajo Technical College decided to serve not just their community college by providing hotspots but also their K-12 schools as well. Funds to help students pay for gas were also provided to students who needed to drive to a hotspot to take classes online or complete assignments (Bray, 2021). Some community colleges were provided an increase in local appropriations after COVID-19, which helped them maintain the financial resources to support online and distance learning (SHEEO, 2021). Additionally, some states utilized their public financial aid funding to subsidize community college students' tuition and fees. Most institutions have now exhausted their federal COVID relief dollars, which resulted in some programs ending while others have been institutionalized.

Learning Modalities

Community colleges have always been creative in how and when they offer classes to meet the needs of diverse student populations. Online learning, whether synchronous (virtual, real-time) or asynchronous (learn on your own time), has been a mainstay at many community colleges where students are attracted to online learning because of its flexibility. While online education may seem counter to the work of a *community* college, this modality aligns with the community college mission of serving diverse student populations, such as working adults who need affordable and flexible options. A student testimonial on Western Wyoming Community College's website underscores how online learning can meet the needs of non-traditional students:

> *I am truly grateful for the online degree option at Western Wyoming Community College! As an older student, they have allowed me to work through my degree, without having to be away from my family or to take time off work. The online platform is easily accessible and very user friendly. Each course has been challenging enough, well planned, straightforward, and highly educational.*
>
> *(Western Wyoming Community College, 2019, para. 1)*

Online and virtual learning has increased among traditional-aged students of all abilities as well, as they too have found these modalities to work well with their schedules and learning needs, especially after the pandemic. To see data regarding states' percentages of students enrolled in distance learning, see https://nces.ed.gov/ipeds/TrendGenerator/app/, then click on Student Enrollment.

Community colleges understand that many students must fit college into their already full and busy lives, which often include jobs, families, and other responsibilities. During the pandemic, community colleges leaned further into their strengths by accelerating their online offerings and expanding *how* they taught their online courses. Community colleges were out in front of asynchronous learning opportunities for their students compared to many four-year colleges and universities because of the necessity of meeting the needs of diverse student populations. Online, asynchronous learning provides additional access to higher education, and some argue that not offering asynchronous courses is prohibitive to many prospective students.

During the fall 2020 and the height of the pandemic, approximately 75% (11.8 million) of all undergraduate students participated in at least one distance education course. Additionally, 44% (7 million) of undergraduate students exclusively pursued distance education courses. Compared to the pre-pandemic fall semester of 2019, a notable increase of 97% in undergraduate students engaged in at least one distance education course (11.8 million versus 6 million). Moreover, the number of students exclusively enrolled in distance education courses experienced a substantial rise in 2020 compared to 2019 (7 million to 2.4 million) (National Center for Education Statistics, 2021).

As noted in Chapter 2, online higher education got its start in tandem with the advent of the public Internet in the 1990s. And while online higher education has proliferated since that time, *all* higher education courses went online in March of 2020. With this dramatic shift to online learning, faculty offered multiple modes of learning online: synchronous and asynchronous. Synchronous courses are like in-person classes where students attend class live through online conferencing platforms such as Zoom, Microsoft

Teams, Google Hangouts, or Webex. Asynchronous learning provides students access to their courses through a learning management system (LMS) platform where they complete work on their own time and per the deadlines outlined by their instructor and course syllabus. Examples of LMS products include Canvas, Blackboard, Moodle, and Google Classroom.

Community college faculty understand that course design is critical to student learning. As such, many institutions employ full-time instructional designers to support faculty members who teach online courses. There is certainly also support for in-person course design, but the online course environment can come with unique and specific challenges related to technology, such as using new software, hardware, and systems—as well as the imperative to follow various policies and laws related to communications, reporting, and copyright. Teaching online can be complex; doing it well is a challenge. One cannot simply move a lecture-based class to an online format. Rather, course and instructional designers work closely with faculty to ensure learning outcomes are achieved in ways accessible to all types of learners to provide quality instruction for every learner. Many institutions use Universal Design for Learning (UDL) and Quality Matters (QM) standards to help develop effective online courses that eliminate student barriers. The UDL framework emphasizes and supports the needs of all learners, including those with disabilities (Robinson & Wizer, 2016). This may include ensuring all videos have captions, all documents are legible to a screen reader, and extra time on quizzes and tests can be accommodated. QM standards address the quality of online and hybrid or blended courses with a faculty-centered peer review process based on best practices for online learning. Students and families should understand that community colleges strive to create online courses designed with every learner in mind. Most courses are reviewed regularly based on student learning outcome data, advances in course design options, and curricular changes.

The demand for online learning has continued at community colleges, though these institutions continue to offer both in-person and online courses to meet the needs of their students. The pandemic accelerated technology adoption in community colleges, improving digital infrastructure and technological capabilities. This has facilitated remote learning and prepared community colleges to integrate technology into their instructional methods even after the pandemic. Some community colleges were committed to making sure their courses were accessible to their local communities by providing free or reduced-rate software such as Adobe Creative Cloud and discounted access to the Internet through providers such as Comcast and AT&T. In California, the community college system used various training opportunities to help students and faculty identify ways to support positive engagement in the virtual setting (Hart et al., 2021). In addition, many institutions began to use the OWL camera, a 360-degree lens that can capture a panoramic view of any space (OWL Labs, 2019) to help groups of people work together effectively in an online meeting space. This easy-to-use device can access Wi-Fi and different video conference software, such as Google Hangouts, Zoom, Webex, and more.

Acknowledging that institutions need a successful online learning process to implement online curricula is essential. Resources to facilitate this process include software *and* hardware. At the onset of COVID-19, institutions had to think critically about how students would access these technologies, how students, faculty, and staff would learn to use the technology, and which strategies were needed to make the implementation process as successful as meeting in person. The California community college system was able to offer personal computers or loanes to faculty, staff, and students to ensure there were equitable resources for everyone to function as in person as possible (Hart et al., 2021). Students seeking online coursework must have strong time management skills, self-motivation, and strong discipline to be successful (Quintana et al., 2005).

On a final note, it is important for students to understand that online education may cost more money. While the cost of online education varies by college often because of program type and sophistication of technology, students may pay an enhanced technology and/or online fee. This important information can be found on an institution's website, typically in the tuition and fees section.

Learning Management Systems (LMSs)

Online learning is largely facilitated through LMSs, such as Canvas or Blackboard. Such systems provide students with real-time assessment, tracking, and grade updates on one platform (Marachi & Quill, 2020). Over 700 LMS programs are used worldwide and across K-12 systems, higher education, and corporate training (Kavitha & Lohani, 2019). These systems allow faculty to use technology, such as audio, video, podcasts, animations, blogs, discussion boards, wikis, polls, quizzes, and more to help engage students in active learning. As previously mentioned, guiding frameworks, such as UDL and QM, are leveraged by faculty and instructional designers to create effective online courses, enhanced by the features of these LMSs—many of which can be accessed through apps, giving students the option to access and complete coursework not only from their computers or laptops, but also from their tablets and/or smartphones. Additionally, most professors who teach using an LMS develop discussion forums, including engaging questions, online and interactive readings, or audio/visual media, so students can actively engage in class discussions, as in an in-person experience. Likely, the local community college uses one of the more common LMSs to support online learning, and it is a good idea for students to learn more about this ahead of enrollment. It should also be noted that many faculty use LMSs alongside their in-person courses as well. This can allow for a paperless classroom experience, meaning students can upload assignments rather than printing them and handing them in and take exams without the need for hard copies or blue books.

Information Security

Turning in assignments online and managing the security of materials may seem uncomfortable to some students, especially those who use technology infrequently. However, institutions have slowly implemented cybersecurity systems to require students, faculty, and staff to utilize login credentials with an identity verification program. Duo Two Factor Authentication is a standard identity and access management security method that requires individuals to accept a push notification to their phone, verifying that they are logging into their educational software.

Community colleges, like banks, medical facilities, and other institutions that handle private or sensitive data are held to the highest data security standards. Offices of Information Security often require regular training for staff and faculty, which covers cybersecurity threats and best practices in protecting sensitive data. Many states have laws that require the attorney general to keep an active list of data breaches. These lists can identify the prevalence of cybersecurity incidents at any given institution. Institutions that participate in Federal Aid programs are subject to the Gramm-Leach-Bliley Act (GLBA) safeguarding rules; see https://www.ftc.gov/business-guidance/privacy-security /gramm-leach-bliley-act. These rules also stipulate that institutions have dedicated cybersecurity staff and a cybersecurity plan. Regular assessment of risk must also take place. GLBA compliance is regularly evaluated by state auditors. Institutions must invest in cybersecurity measures, but how much is invested depends on the institution. Some questions to consider when learning about your college's data privacy and cybersecurity include:

- ◆ Does the institution require multi-factor authentication for staff and students?
- ◆ Do all institutional websites use encryption?
- ◆ Does the institution publish a privacy or data security policy?
- ◆ Does the institution have dedicated cybersecurity personnel such as a Director of Security Operations?
- ◆ Does the institution have a security operations center?
- ◆ Has the institution had one or more data breach incidents in the last year?

Artificial Intelligence

In addition to security, many IT departments have increased their usage of Artificial Intelligence (AI) within their LMSs—and other programs—to help faculty with assessing and tracking grades, providing clear communication, and seeking alternatives for collaborating with other campus partners or groups (Kavitha & Lohani, 2019). Many institutions have invested in systems meant to support student persistence and institutional retention. In other words, the rich algorithms of AI are ultimately meant to help students meet their educational goals and complete credentials. Navigate360 is one such example; see https:// eab.com/solutions/navigate360/. AI is an advanced and evolving technology that can learn, problem-solve, and provide automatic responses based on the information they are integrated with (Somasundaram et al., 2020). With high-tech LMS programs, students can access their classrooms from anywhere in the world with Internet access. AI has helped institutions track software issues promptly, so their systems are not out of order for long periods. Additionally, AI can help "comprehend and detect a person's specific needs to use appropriate pedagogy and enhance the learning process" (Kavitha & Lohani, 2019, p. 698). This is a significant opportunity for institutions to meet students where they are academically rather than providing a one-size-fits-all approach to instruction. AI's advance in teaching and learning has helped students get personalized coaching, advice, and training for career readiness (Somasundaram et al., 2020). Dahl (2023) listed the following eight possible impacts and uses of AI in an LMS:

1. ChatGPT may be used to generate quiz questions, which in the past took a great deal of time for faculty members.
2. A custom homepage widget may also perform a tutoring function in the LMS using the ChatGPT open application programming interface.
3. Chatbots may be placed in the LMS in the content or lessons tool area to facilitate lesson planning.

4. Chatbots may aid with completing coursework and problem-solving at a faster rate than reaching out to faculty.
5. AI may provide pathways that help students learn at their own pace in a more accessible manner.
6. Translations for those with language barriers on classroom content can be facilitated through AI.
7. AI may have the ability to identify course content that may show bias, unnecessary complexity, or ambiguity by the professor before the coursework is published so that it can be addressed.
8. AI can enable speech-to-text applications.

There is a global buzz around the use of AI, and it will greatly impact higher education both inside and outside of the classroom. Exactly how colleges and universities will choose to embrace and help students learn about the new technology is yet to be fully realized.

Big Tech and Student Opportunities

It may be of interest to know that Big Tech companies, such as Amazon and Google, have an increased interest in partnering with community colleges to help train and hire future employees in cybersecurity and other high-need areas. These companies, along with other large technology leaders, such as Salesforce and Cisco, may have particular interest in recruiting high achieving community college students. In November 2021, Microsoft launched an ambitious campaign with two-year colleges to help train and recruit 250,000 people for the U.S. cybersecurity workforce by 2025. In response to that announcement, Connecticut announced all of its state community colleges would begin offering a credit-bearing course that incorporated the Google IT Support certification. The announcement also revealed the state system would offer non-credit short-term training through the partnership. For more information, see: https://workshift.open-campusmedia.org/big-techs-two-year-college-push/. Generally, there is a national push by the tech industry to both hire new workers in fast-growing, high-need areas and to increase employee diversity in these jobs. Partnering with community colleges seems the logical way tech companies can work toward both goals. For additional information regarding industry-led initiatives, such as micro-credentials and certificate programs, at the community college; see Chapter 4.

Increase in Mental Health Concerns

The understanding of and focus on student mental health concerns among higher educational institutions have significantly increased over the past few years especially since the pandemic. For community college students, the stress of going to school while maintaining a steady income and managing life can be overwhelming (Latz, 2023). Consider that community colleges are designed to serve predominantly marginalized students, and many of those students are first-generation students, and some are single parents (Rehr & Nguyen, 2022). This encompasses individuals from various racial/ethnic backgrounds, sexual orientations, gender identities, abilities, citizenship statuses, religions, and more. Such diversity is both the reward and challenge for those working at community colleges across the nation. Research shows that 50% of community college students are experiencing some type of food insecurity, and a little more than that are experiencing housing insecurity (Baker-Smith et al., 2020; Broton et al., 2022). To combat this, some community colleges have developed food pantries where students can access food that has been donated or purchased in the community (Broton & Cady, 2020). And most community colleges regularly connect students with myriad food, housing, childcare, and transportation resources in the local community. It has been noted that both poor mental health (Hysenbegasi et al., 2005; Markoulakis & Kirsh, 2013) and unmet general basic needs (Allen & Allenman, 2019), if left unaddressed, will negatively impact a student's ability to succeed academically. Coupling this with the decrease in community college enrollment, which has resulted in a decline in financial resources for mental health services, community colleges are struggling to keep up with the needs of their students (Rehr & Nguyen, 2022). Approximately 66% of community college students do not use mental health services because they have had negative experiences with previous practitioners before college or because the limited resources have made them inaccessible (Dunbar et al., 2018). Unfortunately, when these mental health concerns are not addressed through therapy, many students show signs of depression and anxiety (Broton et al., 2022).

COVID-19 caused significant challenges for students' physical and mental health, especially during the lockdown(s). Since the pandemic, institutions have slowly started connecting students to more resources and opportunities for mental health services, such as online therapy (Zirkel, 2022). The abrupt shift to online learning caused significant stress for college students—many of whom felt lonely and isolated from their college communities (Liu et al., 2020). In 2021, 33% of community college students reported having significant financial challenges since the pandemic began (CCCSE, 2021). Many struggled to pay for college and had difficulty attending classes or events that did not require social/physical distancing. The inability to pay for college was primarily because of not being able to work during the lockdown and the lack of available job opportunities after the pandemic. Some students or members of their families lost their jobs or were offered fewer working hours (Chin et al., 2022).

Even before the pandemic, institutions connected students to web-based mental health resources, such as online therapy and apps, that provided accessible support for students (Dunbar et al., 2018; Lal & Adair, 2014). Students favored online therapy because of the convenience and accessibility of this resource (Dunbar et al., 2018). In advance of the pandemic, many community colleges hosted preventative programming, increased their counseling services through group therapy or one-off events, and created connections with local therapy services to help bridge the gap with affordability (Lipson et al., 2019). Community college student mental health is and will remain an important issue for community college leaders to consider (Latz, 2023). Every prospective student, including high achieving students, should be keen to learn more about what their local community college has in place to enable mental health support for their student body.

As previously mentioned, COVID-19 resulted in the issuance of emergency funding for technology services and supported students with general emergency funds used to pay bills or address housing insecurity. The stark reality is that food and housing insecurity affects a large proportion of community college students—as many as 61% (The Hope Center for College, Community, and Justice, 2021). The intersection of mental health concerns and challenges related to housing and food security can compound academic struggles among community college students. Despite the evident demand for mental health services in community colleges, a disparity often exists between the need and use of available resources. Community colleges face barriers in securing physical spaces and funding to address mental health concerns and housing and food insecurity. In addition, community college counselors sometimes hold multiple roles, such as academic advising or career coaching, which requires them to balance providing services with a heavy workload. These counselors often also have large caseloads which makes seeking mental health services sometimes even more difficult for students.

Summary

The disruptions caused by the COVID-19 pandemic were felt hard by higher education institutions, including community colleges. However, community colleges demonstrated flexibility and adaptability by quickly transitioning all operations online. This allowed for more continuity in education, where community colleges and their students were less affected by disruptions caused by the pandemic. The crisis accelerated efforts by community colleges to improve their operations and provide better learning experiences. The good news is many programs that arose from the pandemic meant to help students are still in existence. The pandemic accelerated technology integration into community college classrooms, infused emergency federal dollars to jump-start new programs, increased financial support, and emphasized the importance of mental health services for all students. These developments aimed to continue enhancing the learning experiences, promote equity, and support student success. The silver lining of the pandemic is that community colleges were forced to sharpen their ability to offer students support, quality learning opportunities, and technology-infused experiences—all of which may be appreciated by prospective high achieving students.

Discussion and Reflection Prompts

Support Prompts
- ◆ How can you help prepare students for online learning at the community college-level?
- ◆ Where and how can you access information about online learning at your local community college?
- ◆ What unique challenges might students who experienced the pandemic during their K-12 years face throughout the transition to college—and the community college in particular?

Student Prompts
- ◆ How has your idea of going to college changed/not changed following COVID-19?
- ◆ Is online learning a viable option for you? Why, or why not? In what instances might you consider taking online courses?
- ◆ What might help you be successful in an online class? What might be a challenge to you in an online class?

References

Allen, C. C., & Allenman, N. F. (2019). A private struggle at a private institution: Effects of student hunger on social and academic experiences. *Journal of College Student Development, 60*(1), 52–69. https://doi.org/10.1353/csd.2019.0003

Baker-Smith, C., Coca, V., Goldrick-Rab, S., Looker, E., Richardson, B., & Williams, T. (2020). *#RealCollege 2020: Five years of evidence on campus basic need insecurity.* The Hope Center for College, Community, and Justice.

Bray, J. (2021). *Digital divide: How technology access impacts community colleges across the United States during the pandemic.* Association of Community College Trustees.

Broton, K. M., & Cady, C. L. (2020). *Food insecurity on campus: Action and intervention.* Johns Hopkins University Press.

Broton, K. M., Mohebali, M., & Lingo, M. D. (2022). Basic needs insecurity and mental health: Community college students' dual challenges and use of social support. *Community College Review, 50*(4), 456–482. https://doi.org/10.1177/00915521221111460

CCCSE. (2021). The continued impact of COVID-19 on community college students. Available at: https://cccse.org/sites/default/files/CCSSE _COVID.pdf

Chin, J., Mattis, S., Acosta, J., Ramirez, A., Rivera, D., Valadez, A., Leanos, K. B., Jones, I., & Cerezo, A. (2022). "I help my parents by using some of my FAFSA money": A qualitative exploration of pandemic-related stress among community college students. *Community College Journal of Research and Practice,* 1–12. https://doi.org/10.1080/10668926.2022 .2064376

Dahl, B. (2023). How will AI impact the future of the LMS? *Community College Daily.* Available at: https://www.ccdaily.com/2023/04/how -will-ai-impact-the-future-of-the-lms/

Dunbar, M. S., Sontag-Padilla, L., Kase, C. A., Seelam, R., & Stein, B., D. (2018). Unmet mental health treatment need and attitudes toward online mental health services among community college students. *Psychiatric Services, 69*(5), 597–600.

Hart, C. M. D., Xu, D., Hill, M., & Alonso, E. (2021). COVID-19 and community college instructional responses. *Online Learning, 25*(1), 41–69. https:// doi.org/10.24059/olj.v25i1.2568

Hysenbegasi, A., Hass, S. L., & Rowland, C. R. (2005). The impact of depression on the academic productivity of university students. *Journal of Mental Health Policy and Economics, 8*(3), 145–151. http:// www.icmpe.org/test1/journal/issues/v8pdf/8-145_text.pdf

Kavitha, V., & Lohani, R. (2019). A critical study on the use of artificial intelligence, e-Learning technology, and tools to enhance the learners' experience. *Cluster Computing, 22,* 6985–6989. https://doi .org/10.1007/s10586-018-2017-2

Lal, S., & Adair, C. E. (2014). E-mental health: A rapid review of the literature. *Psychiatric Services, 65,* 24–32. https://doi.org/10.1176/appi .ps.201300009

Latz, A. (2023). *Community college student mental health: Faculty experiences and institutional actions.* Rowman & Littlefield.

Lipson, S. K., Lattie, E. G., & Eisenberg, D. (2019). Increased rates of mental health services utilization by U.S. college students: 10-year population-level trends (2007–2017). *Psychiatric Services, 70*(1), 60–63. https://doi.org/10.1176/appi.ps.201800332

Liu, C. H., Pinder-Amaker, S., Hahm, C., & Chen, J. A. (2020). Priorities for addressing the impact of the COVID-19 pandemic on college student mental health. *Journal of American College Health*, 1–3. https://doi.org/10.1080/07448481.2020.1803882

Marachi, R., & Quill, L. (2020). The case of Canvas: Longitudinal datafication through learning management systems. *Teaching in Higher Education, 25*(4), 418–435. https://doi.org/10.1080/13562517.2020.1739641

Markoulakis, R., & Kirsh, B. (2013). Difficulties for university students with mental health problems: A critical interpretive synthesis. *The Review of Higher Education, 37*(1), 77–100. https://doi.org/10.1353/rhe.2013.0073

National Center for Education Statistics. (2021). *Distance learning.* Available at: https://nces.ed.gov/fastfacts/display.asp?id=80

OWL Labs. (2019). What is the Meeting Owl video conferencing camera? Blog. Available at: https://resources.owllabs.com/blog/what-is-the-meeting-owl-video-conferencing-camera#:~:text=The%20Meeting%20Owl%20camera%20is,to%20prevent%20slow%20streaming%20speeds

Quintana, C., Zhang, M., & Krajcik, J. (2005). A framework for supporting metacognitive aspects of online inquiry through software-based scaffolding. *Educational Psychologist, 40*(4), 235–244. https://doi.org/10.1207/s15326985ep4004_5

Rehr, T. L., & Nguyen, D. J. (2022). Approach/avoidance coping among community college students and applications for student affairs professionals. *Journal of Student Affairs Research & Practice, 59*(3), 237–251. https://doi.org/10.1080/19496591.2021.1914641

Robinson, D. E., & Wizer, D. R. (2016). Universal Design for Learning and the Quality Matters guidelines for the design and implementation of online learning events. *International Journal of Technology in Teaching and Learning, 12*(1), 17–32.

SHEEO. (2021). *State higher education finance report.* Available at: https://shef.sheeo.org/report/

Snell, K. (2020, March 26). What's inside the Senate's $2 trillion Coronavirus aid package? *NPR*. https://www.npr.org/2020/03/26/821457551/whats-inside-the-senate-s-2-trillion-coronavirus-aid-package

Somasundaram, M., Mohamed Juaid, K. A., & Mangadu, S. (2020). Artificial intelligence (AI) enabled intelligent quality management system (IQMS) for personalized learning path. *Procedia Computer Science, 172*, 438–442. https://doi.org/10.1016/j.procs.2020.05.096

The Hope Center for College, Community, and Justice. (2021). *#RealCollege 2021: Basic needs insecurity during the ongoing pandemic*. Available at: https://www.luminafoundation.org/wp-content/uploads/2021/04/real-college-2021.pdf

Western Wyoming Community College. (2019). Testimonials. Available at: https://www.westernwyoming.edu/academics/online-learning/testimonials.php

Zirkel, T. (2022). How technology can help community colleges take hold of student outcomes. *Campus Technology*. Available at: https://campustechnology.com/articles/2022/06/24/how-technology-can-help-community-colleges-take-hold-of-student-outcomes.aspx

9

Community College *Is* College

In our discussion about writing this book and as the title suggests, we wanted to break down any biases readers may have about the community college experience and paint a more holistic picture of this important sector of higher education; hence, the title *Community College Is College*. The community college continuum is far-reaching and impacts learners starting in secondary education through CiHS programs and extends through postsecondary education with some community colleges offering bachelor's degrees. As stated throughout this book, the struggle to decide what to do after high school graduation is real and may induce anxiety, fear, excitement, hope, and confusion. High achieving students are not exempt from these struggles. The community college experience may be just what is needed during this transition period as it offers fantastic opportunities for self-discovery and career exploration. The community college may not be the best choice for every student, but it is for many who seek a quality college education that provides flexibility, cost savings, and strong support systems during their early college years. No matter what, prospective college students should seek out and receive accurate information about *all* their postsecondary education options—including the community college. Unfortunately, information about this sector of higher education is often less widely shared and understood.

DOI: 10.4324/9781003346210-9

Throughout this book, we have worked to dispel the notion that community colleges are limited in what they can offer students—even high achieving students. This student population often lacks the critical information they need to decide whether the community college is a viable option on their educational journey. Some of this simply stems from the *four-year push for all* mentality, which is an easier perception to default to when one does not have all the facts and information on hand. Community colleges across the nation offer a wide variety of programs and opportunities for students who may benefit from an experience that in some ways is both similar to and different from four-year institutions. In short, there are alternate experiences and opportunities to those offered at a four-year college or university. Yet, community colleges often suffer from the stigma that they are somehow *less than* and not *real college*. Stigmas develop over time and can be hard to shake. In fact, some community colleges are rebranding themselves by dropping "community" from their name. Against the backdrop of higher education changing nationally mainly because of population shifts, technology advances, the proliferation of online education, and the increased costs of attending college, it is way past time to remove the stigma. It is time to embrace the reality that *community college is college*. Throughout this book, we have sought to dispel misconceptions and provide readers with valuable information to consider. In doing so, we touched on a variety of topics such as the community college's history, college in high school, credentials and degree programs, paying for college, technology, and student life. But what does this all mean? We hope to answer that question with this final chapter by highlighting what life after the community college might look like.

In this final chapter, we emphasize what students can expect from the community college return on investment, which includes robust opportunities and experiences that can lead to transfer and career success. Community colleges offer numerous benefits to their students, providing valuable opportunities and experiences that can positively impact their academic and professional journeys.

Transfer to a Four-Year Institution

For many high achieving students, transferring to a four-year institution and pursuing a bachelor's degree—and then perhaps graduate education—are the ideal next steps after the community college experience. As outlined in Chapter 5, there are many ways community colleges work to facilitate successful transfer experiences for their students, such as college in high school programs, transfer partnerships, and 2+2 articulation agreements. Earning an associate's degree at the community college, then transferring to a four-year institution is a smart way to save money on the way to a bachelor's degree. Moreover, many receiving institutions have on-campus transfer student programs and centers with staffs eager to support students' transition. For example, the University of California, Los Angeles (UCLA) offers a full suite of such opportunities including the following:

- ◆ Transfer Student Center, https://transfers.ucla.edu/
- ◆ Bruin Day for Transfers, https://bruinday.ucla.edu/
- ◆ Transfer Student Living-Learning Community, https://reslife.ucla.edu/living-learning/transfer-experience
- ◆ Center for Community College Partnerships, https://www.aap.ucla.edu/units/cccp/

For high achieving students interested in pursuing a bachelor's degree, starting at the community college may be a the best first step for all kinds of reasons.

Going to Work

Community Partnerships

Local business and industry leaders understand the importance of community colleges, as they know their graduates likely will live and work in their community. Strong partnerships exist between community colleges and local employers, resulting in a pipeline of skilled employees. This relationship benefits local employers who may have numerous vacant positions or high employee turnover. It is a win-win for graduates and the community, as graduates of community colleges are often committed to remaining in their local communities because of strong and enduring familial and community ties. Community employer and community college partnerships can benefit students and the community in a specific location.

For example, in Louisville, Kentucky, the United Postal Service (UPS) formed a partnership to help fill the need for local worker shortages. UPS Airlines is the second largest cargo airline in the world based on freight volume and one of the largest employers in Kentucky. Because of its central geographical location, Louisville is a major distribution hub for the country. UPS decided to create a pathway for employees to continue their education and fulfill their job responsibilities at their distribution center. As a result, a partnership was created, allowing employees to enroll in Jefferson Community and Technical College working in partnership with the University of Louisville. This custom-designed partnership is known as Metropolitan College. Students attending Metropolitan College work the third shift as package handlers for UPS Worldport in Louisville, Kentucky. Students are paid a wage and given free tuition at either the University of Louisville or Jefferson Community and Technical College. Students can earn bonuses for their academic progress and earn a debt-free degree, which could be a boon for high achieving students. Metropolitan College degrees range from K-12 teaching certifications, healthcare degrees, automotive technician, plus many other choices. In addition, students can earn technology micro-credentials from Google, IBM, and Microsoft. This partnership is a win-win for both UPS and students. Before the UPS Metropolitan College partnership, third-shift workers at UPS stayed, on average, for eight weeks. Once the college students joined the third-shift workforce, the retention rate jumped to 200 weeks. This is a considerable cost saving for UPS as they do not have to train new employees every eight weeks. In turn, students expand their employment opportunities, and Kentucky garners a better-equipped workforce. Over the last 25 years, Metropolitan College has supported 23,000 students to attend college debt-free and 13,000 degrees and certificates have been earned. For more information, see https://metro-college.com/. Corporate partnerships are just one of the ways that community colleges have become innovative in offering meaningful educational opportunities with little or no student debt to build better futures for their students and a strong workforce for their communities.

Corporate Sponsors and College-to-Career Bridge Programs

Corporations have implemented a variety of innovative ways to help college students transition into career pathways. Many organizations have created College-to-Career bridge programs to help students gain full-time jobs (see https://www.bestcolleges .com/blog/career-bridge-programs/explore/). These programs can vary greatly from one employer to the next. Programs can last from a few months up to a few years. We have included a few examples here, but there are many more available opportunities:

- ◆ Texas Instruments invites community college graduates to apply for their rotation programs. This program allows recent graduates to work within different areas at the company to understand employment options. The variety of experiences allows graduates to meet and work with other employees to better see potential career paths. For more information, see https://careers.ti.com/ students/.
- ◆ Honeywell offers a similar program called Honeywell's PMT Early Career Engineer Rotational Program (ECERP). This program offers recent community college graduates hands-on experience working within various functional and business areas in the company for up to three years. At the end of the rotational program, the participants may move into a full-time position at a Honeywell site. For more information, see https://careers.honeywell.com /us/en/job/P-100003/Early-Career-Engineering-Rotation -Program-ECERP-Engineer.
- ◆ Cigna Healthcare offers internship positions and rotational programs for undergraduate and graduate students. They also offer leadership development programs

for recent graduates to help develop the skills necessary to advance their careers. For more information, see https:// jobs.thecignagroup.com/us/en/studentandgraduates.

Civil Service Employment

Historically, civil service jobs have provided dependable career paths for many Americans. These positions entail working for the government in a department or agency at the local, state, or federal level. Examples include working for a Department of Transportation, Department of Health, or Department of Human Services. Community college graduates ought to consider government jobs as an option when planning careers. The U.S. federal government offers opportunities for students to complete paid internships while attending college. There are several programs to assist students and recent college graduates in finding internship opportunities with the federal government. For example, the Pathways Program (see https://www.usajobs.gov/ Help/working-in-government/unique-hiring-paths/students/) includes several routes to connect with employment opportunities in the civil service.

Work-Based Learning and Co-Ops

Community college students often engage in experiential learning activities, which employers consider valuable. Activities such as internships, practicums, and volunteerism are examples of experiential learning. And these experiences lead to jobs. Students who leave community colleges with experiential learning and a strong base of skills and competencies will have a leg-up on employment. Additional information on the competencies sought by employers can be found on the National Association of Colleges and Employers (NACE) website; see https://www .naceweb.org/career-readiness/competencies/career-readiness-defined. NACE outlines the following key competencies: Career & Self-Development; Communication; Critical Thinking; Equity & Inclusion; Leadership; Professionalism; Teamwork; and Technology. A quick look at the academic offerings at any community college will reveal that their graduates gain skills and competencies critical for both work and life.

Work-Based Learning (WBL) and cooperative learning (Co-Ops) are additional examples of experiential learning opportunities meant to integrate learning in class and on the job. These opportunities connect students' curriculum to the real world. Students practice skills and observe professionals completing the work in fields they are preparing to enter. Much of a student's learning in WBL is through job shadowing, mentorship, service learning, volunteering, paid work experience, and more. WBL can resemble an internship or research project for class credit, with limited on-site hours required to complete, so students are not overextended while attending college.

Wake Technical Community College in North Carolina provides a good example of WBL; see https://www.waketech.edu/programs-courses/credit/work-based-learning. WBL creates an opportunity where students can immediately and directly apply what they have learned in courses to their workplace. Students can apply their communication, problem-solving, interpersonal, and informational processing skills to their jobs, which can provide instant validation of skills and knowledge sets learned in classes. WBL fosters readiness for students to enter the workforce and begin their careers. Having true hands-on experience makes them more marketable in the job market. Sandhills Community College—also in North Carolina—offers WBL in a variety of areas, including Geomatics Technology, Civil Engineering Technology, Therapeutic Massage, and Landscape Gardening. For more information, see https://www.sandhills.edu/faculty-staff/work-based-learning-forms.html.

Cooperative learning opportunities, or Co-Ops, are another form of experiential learning. Co-Ops require partnership and clear communication between students, the community college, and employers. Co-Ops have many benefits for each party—as well as the community in which the cooperative learning program takes place. That said, each party has specific responsibilities and expectations to uphold for the Co-Op to work well. Calhoun Community College in Alabama provides a good example; see https://calhoun.edu/student-services/career-services/cooperative-learning/. Through Co-Ops, students can gain meaningful work experience while in college, which is especially important in a competitive job market.

Entrepreneurship

Entrepreneurship is becoming a career choice for a growing number of people around the world. Entrepreneurs are developing businesses that offer jobs to others in the community. Investment helps provide local, state, and federal economic stability and growth in entrepreneurship. Therefore, we are compelled to address entrepreneurship as a post-college opportunity. To meet the entrepreneurial demand, many colleges and universities have established entrepreneurship programs to help students gain the knowledge and skills to start their businesses. Cornell University provides an example; see https://www.colgate.edu/success-after-colgate/career-development/finding-career-path/industries-careers/career-paths-5.

Community colleges also support the growth of entrepreneurship as a field of study and vocation in a variety of ways. For example, Motlow State Community College in Tennessee offers an Associate of Applied Science degree in Business with a concentration in Entrepreneurship. See https://www.motlow.edu/academics/programs/business-technology/entrepreneurship.html for details. Many community colleges also house small business incubators such as the Entrepreneurship Center at Central Community College in Nebraska; see https://www.cccneb.edu/entrepreneurship-center. Some community colleges also offer ongoing resources to small business owners. For example, Washtenaw Community College in Michigan joined the Michigan Small Business Association to provide added training and support to Small Business Association members. This partnership helps community college graduates who wish to start their own businesses.

Often, because entrepreneurial endeavors touch all workforce sectors, entrepreneurship courses can be taken in conjunction with other degrees, such as business or culinary programs. There are many different types of entrepreneurs and startup companies that offer a variety of job opportunities, including, but not limited to product development, software engineering, branding and brand promotion, freelancing, and marketing. For example, a student may choose to earn an associate degree in Culinary Arts while also integrating entrepreneurship courses into their degree plan. Such an educational background could well equip that student to open their own catering company. In another example, a student may be seeking a degree in Early Childhood Education, yet also taking entrepreneurship courses as part of their curriculum. In this example, the two-year program could be beneficial to the aspiring daycare center owner. The message seems clear here—community colleges help prepare students by providing the skills and supportive networks necessary to create entrepreneurial ventures.

The National Association for Community College Entrepreneurship (NACCE) is a national organization that supports colleges as they co-create new programs with corporate and education partners. More than 400 community and technical colleges across the U.S. are members of NACCE, indicating the importance of entrepreneurship education for students and graduates. This organization offers training, information, seminars, and webinars to inform community college leaders and educators about the importance of innovative entrepreneurship education at the community college. For more information regarding NACCE, see https://www.nacce.com.

Maker Spaces are another resource at some community colleges. These on-campus spaces provide students with opportunities for hands-on design and experimentation using a variety of tools and technology. For example, Sussex County Community College in Newton, New Jersey, recently opened its New Academic Center and Maker Space. The highlight of this building is its Maker Space, which was designed for innovative hands-on learning; it contains high-tech and low-tech machines to create an environment that promotes creativity, critical thinking, problem-solving, and product prototyping. Tools such as 3D printers, laser cutters, robotics, scanners, and other equipment allow students to experiment and learn skills to advance their careers. Whether students graduate with a degree in 3D Computer Arts,

Fashion Design, or Optics Technology, the lessons learned in the Maker Space will help them consider entrepreneurship as a career path. For more information, see https://www.usaarchitects.com/project/new-academic-center-and-maker-space. Access to these creative spaces where ideas and innovation meet and come alive may be of special interest to high achieving students. See https://makerspace.com to learn more.

Notable Community College Alumni

To help fight the stigma, community colleges would be wise to better spotlight their high achieving graduates, as there are many. These notable alumni shine an important light on what is possible by attending a community college. Just as four-year colleges and universities have famous alumni, so do community colleges. For example, long-time award-winning actor Morgan Freeman attended Los Angeles (LA) City College because he wanted to become an actor. Known for his unique voice and ability to create a presence on screen, Freeman credits his college diction teacher for helping him gain the skills needed to be a great actor. On *Jimmy Kimmel Live* in 2016, Freeman said, "I went to school [LA City College] to study how to be an actor; I had a voice and diction instructor who was very good at his job." To view this clip, see https://www.youtube.com/watch?v=avAB-So6xpqg. Freeman went on to develop a highly successful acting career spanning multiple decades, and he credits a teacher at a community college for helping develop some of the necessary skills. *U.S. News and World Report* highlighted several notable people who have attended two-year institutions. That list can be found at: https://www.usnews.com/education/community-colleges/slideshows/famous-people-who-attended-community-college?onepage.

The California Community Colleges Chancellor's Office lists many notable people with California Community College educational backgrounds on its website. The full list can be found at: https://www.cccco.edu/About-Us/Notable-Alumni. This list includes former California Governor Arnold Schwarzenegger, J. Craig Venter, a twenty-first-century leading scientist in genomic research, famed Hollywood director George Lucas, notable actor and comedian Robin Williams, plus many more.

While community colleges may not always have robust offices of alumni affairs in the same way four-year institutions do, there are many success stories that can, and should be, shared. For the community colleges that do have alumni associations, they often offer various ways alumni can give back to their two-year alma mater. The City Colleges of Chicago offer an example; see https://www.ccc.edu/site/pages/alumni_association.aspx. Success stories among famous community college graduates are plenty, but even more importantly, the *successful* community college graduate may be around the corner—ask family members, neighbors, nurses, doctors, welders, day care owners, and chief executive officers where they got their start in college, and we can assure you, many will say at their local community college.

Alex's Community College Story

To illustrate the main themes within this book, here we would like to share Alex's fictional—but typical—narrative about a student who chose to attend community college and their success story to showcase how community college *is* college and how the institution could be a destination for high achieving students. We hope this narrative provides a solid visual on which to reflect and process the information in this book.

Alex's Story

Alex was a very motivated and high achieving high school senior interested in earning a college degree but did not know where to start. He had a strong high school GPA, plus he had taken AP and dual credit courses in high school, which gave him confidence that he could succeed in college; however, he struggled with understanding his higher education options as he would be the first in his family to attend college. His family was always supportive of his goals but could not offer much in the way of advice or information about college in general. Affording tuition along with room and board at the large public university closest to him, was even harder for Alex to wrap his head around as his family had very limited financial resources. He knew friends who were planning to take out large loans to help pay for their college, but Alex did not want to do that. After a great deal of online research regarding the schools he thought he *should* attend, he finally talked with his high school counselor who recommended an alternative where he *could* attend— his local community college. During a campus visit which included lunch at the Student Center, Alex learned about his academic options at XYZ Community College, which included the opportunity to take classes in the Honors College, join student clubs and organizations, and hang out in the MakerSpace. Considering the cost savings he would realize, along with the transfer-ability of his honors credits, flexible class schedules, and active student life opportunities, Alex enrolled. Community college had not been on Alex's radar. But once enrolled, Alex quickly realized he had made the best choice. Frankly, it was the right choice.

With a strong work ethic and desire to succeed, Alex dove headfirst into the college experience. He took full advantage of the resources available at the community college. The dedicated faculty and staff provided excellent support and guidance, helping Alex transition smoothly from high school to college. He loved many of his faculty members and met with them often during office hours. He also knew some high school friends who had transferred to the community college after a tough first semester at the four-year institution. One of Alex's friends, Kate, needed a semester or two to improve her grades and to live closer to home. Kate talked about feeling isolated and overwhelmed at her university, while Alex developed close relationships with his peers in the Honors College and with his community college professors who encouraged him throughout his academic journey. Alex joined clubs and organizations that matched his academic and personal interests. These extracurricular activities allowed Alex to develop leadership skills and foster meaningful connections with other students. Additionally, with encouragement from his advisors and faculty members, Alex sought internships and volunteer opportunities in the local community, where he gained practical experiences and expanded his network. Recognizing the importance of academic excellence, Alex shined in the honors program where he built a strong transfer resume with excellent grades and rigorous courses. This commitment to learning was noticed, and Alex was awarded several scholarships based on academic achievement and demonstrated leadership abilities. The financial burden of education was manageable for Alex and his family because he chose to go to community college. The lower costs allowed Alex to focus on his studies without additional stress. Unlike many of his friends, Alex saved money during his first two years of college which he could apply to his remaining two years once he transferred to the university. He also hoped some of the savings could go toward his future graduate studies.

As the time to transfer to a university approached, Alex researched potential institutions and sought guidance from his community college academic and transfer advisors. He carefully curated his college applications, highlighting his achievements, experiences, and personal growth as an honors student at the community college. With a solid academic record, impressive extra and co-curricular involvement, and well-crafted essays, Alex received acceptance letters to his top universities. As stated earlier, his experiences at the community college—both academic and co-curricular—helped Alex build an excellent transfer resume, which also helped him get accepted into a prestigious four-year institution. Could this high achieving student have been successful straight away after high school at the four-year institution? Likely, but what the community college experience did offer him in terms of financial savings and preparation for transfer was significant. His hard work paid off, and he was offered scholarships and financial aid packages from several four-year institutions. Ultimately, Alex chose to attend the prestigious four-year institution, which offered sufficient financial aid, fulfilling his dreams of continuing his postsecondary education journey. Alex continued to thrive academically at the university and actively participated in campus activities. The foundation built during his time at the community college prepared him well for the challenges of university life. He graduated with honors, earning a degree in his chosen field.

After completing his bachelor's degree, Alex pondered on going to graduate school but decided to first seek employment. Graduate school could wait and perhaps be paid for by his future employer. The skills, knowledge, and network of mentors Alex had developed during his community college and university years proved invaluable in securing meaningful job opportunities. Alex's perseverance, determination, and ability to seize opportunities paved the way for success. Alex's story is an inspiring one but it is not an anomaly. Alex is like many high achieving high school students who are first-generation and may face financial barriers to attending a university upon graduating from high school. Alex's story demonstrates that attending a community college can be the first step to a bright future, offering a supportive platform for personal growth, academic achievement, and a pathway to achieving big dreams.

Benefits of the Community College Option

To bring this book to a close, here we recap the benefits of the community college option for high achieving students.

Cost Savings

We must start with cost. Community colleges are typically more affordable than but not inferior to four-year institutions, making them an attractive option for students who want to save on tuition and fees. This affordability can help reduce student loan debt and/or allow students to work part-time instead of full-time while attending college. High school students can take extra advantage of cost savings by enrolling in community college courses while still in high school and earning college credit.

Accessibility and Flexibility

Community colleges are conveniently located, making them easily accessible for students who live in the area. This accessibility eliminates the need for students to relocate or commute long distances, saving time and money. These institutions typically offer various class schedules, including evening, weekend, and online courses. This flexibility allows students to balance their education with other commitments such as family, work, or personal responsibilities.

Acting as a Bridge

Community colleges can serve as a bridge between high school and a four-year institution. They provide a supportive and less overwhelming environment for students to adapt to the academic expectations of college life. High school students can experience college-level coursework and develop the skills necessary to succeed in higher education. Community colleges typically have smaller class sizes compared to four-year institutions. This smaller student-to-faculty ratio gives students more personalized attention from faculty, fostering a supportive learning environment and allowing for more significant interaction and engagement in the classroom—and beyond. High school students who decide to attend a community college can benefit from close interactions with faculty and staff, who are dedicated to helping students succeed. This level of support can enhance a student's learning experience and boost their confidence. Furthermore, many community college faculty are part-time instructors with full-time jobs in the community. Students not only learn course content, but they also enrich their resume-building connections and future employment prospects by building rapport with these faculty. Many community college students find these local relationships invaluable as they advance their careers.

Resources

Community colleges typically offer comprehensive support services, including academic advising, tutoring, career counseling, and financial aid assistance. These resources help students navigate their educational journey and address any challenges they may experience along the way. Students can benefit from these services while gaining valuable insights and guidance as they decide on their next steps after attending a community college. Graduates may choose to transfer to a four-year institution, some choose to enter the world of work, some start their own businesses. Simply put, the options are endless.

Sense of Belonging

A significant benefit of attending college may be experiencing a sense of belonging and developing connections with a community of people throughout the educational journey. These bonds often lead to life-long friendships, support networks, mentors, and sponsors. Another advantage of the community college experience is that there are opportunities to interact with and learn from a diverse student body. Community colleges serve an incredibly diverse student population, which gives students the opportunities to understand differences, challenge biases, and experience the beautiful tapestry that makes up humanity.

Summary

Community colleges can offer high achieving high school students a cost-effective, supportive, and academically enriching environment. By taking advantage of the many opportunities available, students can gain a head start on their college education, explore various career paths, and develop the skills necessary for future success. Students choosing to attend community colleges will benefit from a wide variety of experiences that help students build confidence, cultivate community, and gain a sense of belonging.

Talk with people who attended a community college, and listen to the many different stories, as each journey is as unique as the community college itself. Some students attach strongly to their two-year institutions, while others may think of their time at the community college as a stepping-stone to a better job or a bachelor's degree. Regardless of the disparate student experiences, one thing holds true: community colleges are designed to serve *all* students—including high achieving students—and help students reach their goals, whatever they may be, whenever they wish to attend, and however they wish to take classes. While community colleges are complex institutions in that they serve so many, and in so many ways, their mission to serve and educate students is a constant.

We encourage all readers to consider how the local community college might meet the needs of motivated and high achieving students.

Discussion and Reflection Prompts

Support Prompts
- ◆ What are your major take-aways from this book?
- ◆ Among those with whom you interact, who do you feel would most benefit from reading this book?
- ◆ What are some actions you can take today to further support the high achieving students with whom you work to learn more about the community college?
- ◆ In what ways has this book challenged your assumptions about the community college sector?

Student Prompts
- ◆ What are your overall thoughts about community colleges? Have they changed since reading this book? If so, in what ways? Does your circle of friends compare where they have been accepted and which college or university they wish to attend? If so, would you be more comfortable telling them you are starting at a community college after reading this book? If yes, why, and if no, why not?
- ◆ What are your goals, intentions, and dreams? How might your local community college help you reach your goals, stay true to your intentions, and live out your dreams?

Printed in the United States
by Baker & Taylor Publisher Services